EMPOWERED WOMAN

Five Principles for
Living Your Best Life
and Fulfilling Your Potential

ADEBOLA AJAO, Ph.D.

Free Gift

To say thank you for buying my book, go to
https://www.adebolaajao.com/ and enter your
name and email in "Contact Me" to get a free
copy of the Empowered Woman Planner and
Gratitude Journal I created as a companion to
Empowered Woman.

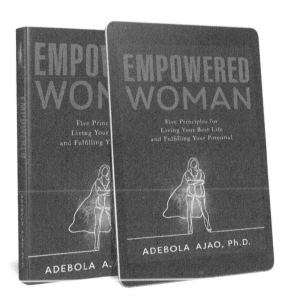

Dedication

This book is dedicated to my mother, all the women who have inspired me along my journey, and women around the world who aspire to live their best life and maximize their potential.

Special Thanks

To my parents, Stephen and Eunice Olanrewaju
who believed in me and gave everything
to raise me into a successful adult.

To my partner for his love, support, and
commitment to our marriage and family.

To my children Dara, Jola, and Timi, for making me
their mama and their constant love and laughter.

Author's Service Commitment to Readers

Ten percent of all proceeds from this book will go to help support and empower young women as part of the author's family foundation Adegoke Olanrewaju Foundation. The foundation has been operating and doing charity work in Nigeria, West Africa for over ten years.

The foundation is committed to improving the lives of others through educational scholarships, financing of small businesses, and improving food insecurity in local communities.

By buying and reading this book, you are being of service to yourself and others and making the world a better place.

Table of Contents

Introduction

There is no limit to what we as women can accomplish.
—Michelle Obama

Who is an empowered woman?

An empowered woman is a visionary woman—a woman who takes control of her life, creates a vision for her future, believes in her abilities, and is determined to achieve her dreams.

An empowered woman is willing to take risks, is focused on her goals, works hard to get what she wants, perseveres through challenges, and finds the right resources to get to her destination.

An empowered woman is determined to keep growing, leverages her talents, passion, skills, and experiences to create her future. She says yes to the right opportunities and is not afraid to try new things.

An empowered woman knows her limitations and works to overcome them. She is not perfect, but she is not deterred by disappointments and set-backs. She learns from her mistakes and keeps moving forward with her goals.

An empowered woman surrounds herself with other empowered women who are examples to her and encourage her along the way. An empowered woman lifts other women up and helps them achieve their own dreams.

If this sounds like who you are or who you want to be, this book is for you. If you are ready to break down all barriers of self-doubt, overcome all forms of insecurity and stagnancy, unlock your potential, and be empowered to crush your goals, then keep on reading. I wrote this book to inspire ordinary women who aspire to be extraordinary. This book provides practical tools for women who are ready for a breakthrough in their professional and personal lives, who want to leave a legacy, and who are determined to leave this world better than how they met it.

Allow me to introduce myself. I was born in Nigeria, West Africa into a middle-class family, the first of five children. As a first child, my parents instilled leadership qualities in me and taught me to always lead my siblings by example. Like most Nigerians, I had a large extended family with countless uncles, aunties, and cousins, so my upbringing instilled in me the love of family and the spirit of bringing people together.

I was born into a family of educators. My father was an economics professor at a national university and my mother was a high school principal. They both taught me to aim high and work hard as education is the greatest equalizer. I was a studious young person and excelled academically, so it was no surprise that I wanted to become a scientist and later pursued a doctoral degree following in my father's footsteps.

Based on my family background and upbringing, the first thirty years of my life felt fairly predictable. My parents provided a lot of guidance and financial support for my education through my master's degree level, so I did not have to struggle much in my earlier years of life other than staying focused on my studies. I spent the first fifteen years of my life completing my elementary, middle, and high school education in Nigeria. Then I moved to the United Kingdom for two years of advanced level post-secondary education. After that, I moved to the United States of America for college, where I attended both the University of New Orleans and Purdue University for my Bachelor of Science degree. After my first degree, I decided to pursue a master's degree in public health with a specialty in epidemiology and biostatistics. I moved to Boston, Massachusetts for my master's degree where I met my husband. We lived and worked in Boston for four years before getting married and deciding to relocate to Maryland for work.

The move to Maryland brought new work opportunities for us. I got a position with the University of Maryland to go back to my home country, Nigeria, as part of a team setting up an HIV prevention and treatment program. This was the beginning of the HIV pandemic and the United States gave a lot of money to Africa to fight HIV. I had the opportunity to work in Nigeria six months every year as part of the team that helped build an HIV prevention, testing, and treatment program. I spent long days in the sun with my team in different parts of Nigeria, taking HIV testing to people that would not have been tested otherwise, listening to their stories, educating them about practical ways to prevent HIV, and referring HIV positive patients to free United States government funded HIV treatment. In this position, I was also engaged in HIV research activities, which opened my mind to future possibilities as a public health researcher.

As a public health professional, I was empowered by the stories of the people I had the privilege to meet and impact on the job. This opportunity was by far one of the most rewarding work experiences of my life. After two years of this life-changing work experience, I decided to return to school to pursue my doctoral degree in epidemiology and start my family at the same time.

Ten years later, about the time I turned forty years old, I reached a crossroad in my life. Up until that point, I felt like I had a fairly straightforward path in life, and I was quite comfortable navigating my life path. At this crossroad, I started to ask myself what the next chapter of my life would look like. I was thirteen years into my marriage, ten years into my career as an epidemiologist, and ten years into motherhood raising our three children. At this crossroad, I started feeling stagnant with my personal and financial growth potential. I knew there was much more I could accomplish but I was not sure what and how. Professionally, I would have to make drastic changes, but I was not quite poised to make the type of change necessary due to my family obligations. This was a turning point for me. A point where I did not feel confident about the next chapter of my professional life, but I knew I was capable of much more and I had to figure out my new future opportunities. I started to self-reflect and think deeply about my talents, skills, knowledge, experiences, and what I enjoy doing. This opened up my mind to new and creative professional and personal opportunities different from where I previously allowed my mind to go. I realized that the new landscape of possibilities was limitless but also challenging, and I must face my fears of unfamiliar opportunities and unchartered territories in order to explore new possibilities. I also realized I needed proven practical tools to navigate my new future possibilities and succeed on my new journey.

This book is a collection of the principles and practical tools I have collected along the way and I continue to collect and use on my life journey to maximize my potential as a professional, wife, and mother. In the first section of this book, I review the five principles necessary to achieve any life goal. In the second section, I use my personal stories to demonstrate how I have used these principles to tackle and achieve my goals in my professional, motherhood, marital, and financial life. Lastly, I provide additional practical ways to use the five principles to tackle your goals in the different areas of your life as a woman. Although my focus is on women, these principles are universal and can be applied by both genders. This book is short, easy to read, and practical. I use reader friendly format of short paragraphs and bullet points, allowing you to easily apply each principle to your individual situation.

Using these principles on my journey made me believe I can do anything I put my mind to while balancing my professional and family responsibilities. Using these principles, I feel empowered and confident to tackle any goal. I am no longer afraid to pursue new opportunities, and I no longer feel like any goal is impossible. Even though I still have a long road ahead of me, my journey so far has inspired me to empower other women by teaching them that they can do the same.

I used several of these principles when writing this very book, so the fact that you are reading it is a testament to the power of these principles. If you take the practical steps described in this book, you are guaranteed results. You will begin to take charge of your destiny, conquer your fears, and gain the confidence you need to tackle your goals—you will never see things the same way again. You will begin to build your legacy and journey into your future of unlimited possibilities. If you do not take the steps described in this book, you will leave your destiny in the hands of others, stagnate your progress in life, and continue to wonder why others are succeeding more than you.

This book was written during the COVID-19 pandemic, a time when many lost loved ones, and many lost their livelihood. A time when many suffered loneliness, depression, and abuse due to the social distancing measures put in place to prevent the spread of the virus. On the other hand, the pandemic could be seen as a blessing—a time of great reflection, and a call to action. A call to rise up and take charge of your personal, professional, financial, and family life. A time I realized you and I can no longer stand by and leave our lives and destinies in the hands of others. Whether you are reading this book during the COVID-19 pandemic or years afterward (in, hopefully, a COVID-free world), the principles discussed here are timeless and will always be relevant and useful. Take inspiration from this determined woman who fought through this difficult time and came out on the other side even stronger than before.

For more empowering messages, follow me on:

Instagram:
https://www.instagram.com/empowered.woman2021/

YouTube:
https://www.youtube.com/channel/
UCH7B5TDKS9san0KD0bulA6w/featured

There is no force more powerful than a woman determined to rise.
–Dorothy Dandridge

SECTION 1

Find Your Purpose, Change Your Mindset, and Fulfill Your Potential

The best way to predict your future is to create it.
–Abraham Lincoln

Find Your Purpose

You are gifted. I am gifted. We all have special gifts and inborn talents that we need to unlock. *Talent* is a person's "natural endowment or natural ability to be good at a particular activity without being taught or with minimal practice."[1,2]

Traditionally, talents are seen as creative, artistic, athletic, or mental abilities. Besides being an academic genius, an athletic star, or a famous singer, actor, photographer, or designer, there are many other forms of talents that are not as easily recognized.

Growing up, I did not feel like I had any talents. I was not creative, and I could not draw, paint, sing, or play an instrument. I was not athletic, and I did not play any sport. As an adult, over time, I started to take note of the things I do well. First, I realized that I am a logical, critical, and systematic thinker. Second, I possess emotional intelligence, I am in touch with my emotions and the emotions of others around me. Third, I am empathetic and I like to listen and advise others regarding their challenges and struggles. Fourth, I am a natural leader. I am the first of five children and I like to lead by example.

At first glance, these attributes may not be easily recognized as talents, but these are attributes we are either gifted

---

[1] "Talent," Merriam-Webster (Merriam-Webster, n.d.), accessed 2021, https://www.merriam-webster.com/dictionary/talent.

[2] "TALENT: Definition in the Cambridge English Dictionary,"TALENT | definition in the Cambridge English Dictionary (Cambridge University Press, n.d.), accessed 2021, https://dictionary.cambridge.org/us/dictionary/english/talent.

with or have developed over time and can use to our advantage. We can leverage what we have such as our talents, passion, strength, skills, knowledge, and experiences to create our future and get to our destination.

Here are a few more examples and brief descriptions of talents that may not be easily recognized.

- Adaptability: ability to adjust to new conditions or situations
- Creativity: ability to imagine new things or see things in new ways
- Communication: ability to clearly convey information to others
- Confidence: ability to believe in one's own abilities
- Critical Thinking: ability to objectively evaluate facts to form judgement
- Entrepreneurship: ability to take risks to create and manage a business to create wealth
- Emotional intelligence: ability to recognize and manage self-emotion and emotion of others
- Empathy: ability to understand and share the emotions of others
- Enthusiasm: ability to get excited about new tasks and challenges
- Extrovert: ability to be social and outgoing at all times
- Inquisitiveness: ability to be curious and ask relevant questions
- Leadership: ability to influence and motivate others toward a common goal.
- Listening: ability to accurately receive and interpret information

- Logical: ability to think systematically and analytically
- Networking: ability to seek and develop new social and professional relationships
- Optimism: ability to be hopeful and always see the positive in everything
- Perseverance: ability to continue taking action despite difficulty or delay in achieving success
- Persistence: ability to be determined to achieve a goal despite difficulties or obstacles
- Problem solving: ability to find solutions to difficult or complex issues
- Public speaking: ability to engage and speak to large audiences without fear or anxiety
- Resilience: ability to recover quickly from set-backs

This is not an exhaustive list but is a starting point to help you start to recognize and identify your hidden talents. One book useful for discovering your talents is *Now Discover your Strengths* by Marcus Buckingham and Donald Clifton. Other examples of not so recognizable talents can also be found online.[3]

It is important to identify and maximize your talents to reach your potential. Now, dig deep within yourself and reflect on your talents, skills, strengths, passion, experiences, desires, and favorite things to do. Your talents are unique to you so be authentic and honest with yourself as you reflect to identify your talents. Although many talents are natural,

---

[3] Michael Hartzell, "Howto-6-List of Strengths & Talents You May Have," michaelhartzell (MICHAEL HARTZELL INTERNATIONAL, n.d.), accessed 2021, https://www.michaelhartzell.com/Blog/bid/17550/Howto-6-List-of-Strengths-Talents-You-May-Have.

they can also be acquired over time so be open to identifying new talents as you continue on your life journey.

Here are some practical ways to help you get started with identifying your talents.

- Write down your daily thoughts and activities in a journal. After a while, you will start to see a pattern in your interests and activities.
- Make a list of the things you are naturally good at and the things you enjoy doing to start to identify your talents.
- Take note of what people say about you and the adjectives others use to describe you.
- List individuals you admire and identify the talents you admire in them as you likely admire talents you identify with.
- If you are jealous of talents you see in others, make a note of these talents as you likely have similar talents you have not explored or maximized.

Next, order your talents from strongest to weakest. Then identify new opportunities that align with your strongest talents first. This is an important recipe for success. Success comes when you do what you love, and you love what you do. Follow your passion and talents, turn them into your purpose, and let your purpose take you to your life destination.

However, this process does not happen overnight. It is a continuous process of self-reflection and self-realization that leads to finding your purpose. Talents can also evolve with time and experience, so be open to discovering new talents as you grow.

The meaning of life is to find your gift, the
purpose of life is to give it away.
–William Shakespeare

Change Your Mindset and Fulfill Your Potential

Now, it is time to prepare your mind for the journey ahead. After identifying your talents, identify new opportunities that align with your talents, and create goals for maximizing these opportunities.

In the next section, we will discuss the five principles you need to prepare your mind, develop a plan, and conquer your goals. Each of these principles is deep by itself and famous authors have written books about each one of them. Adhere to the five principles below to develop the right mindset and action plan to embark on your success journey and accomplish your goals.

1. Think Big
2. Conquer Your Fears
4. Seek and Acquire Knowledge
5. Find Mentors
6. And finally, Act and Follow Through

Each principle is a step that leads into the next principle creating an empowerment feedback loop as illustrated in the figure.

Practicing the first principle of "Thinking Big" gives you the courage to "Conquer Your Fears". Taking steps to "Conquer Your Fears" strengthens your desire to "Seek and

Acquire Knowledge". "Seeking and Acquiring Knowledge" shows you the importance of "Finding Mentors". "Finding Mentors" allows you to learn from others who have made their dreams possible and propels you to "Act and Follow-through" with your own goal(s). Conquering one goal at a time allows you to "Think Bigger" about your future goals continuing the empowerment feedback loop.

The Empowerment Feedback Loop

If you are further along in your life journey, you may be wondering if these principles still apply to you. No matter where you are along your life journey, it is never too late to apply these principles to your goals. In the next sections, I provide an overview of each principle and practical ways to actualize and master these principles.

> Everything in life starts with your mindset first and your actions second. Your actions follow your thoughts, your beliefs, and ideas. To make a shift, to free your energy, start with getting your mind right: and then, take action.
> –Sylvester Mcnutt III

Think Big

It all begins and ends with our mind. What you
give power to has power over you.
–Leon Brown

The Power of Your Mind

Your mind is your greatest asset and provides your cognitive
ability to think, imagine, perceive, and judge. Everything
starts and ends with your mind. After identifying your talents, use your mind to your advantage by thinking big about
what you want to achieve with your talents.

When you think big, you can break barriers and create
new opportunities with your mind. When you think big,
you can visualize your potential achievement on a mas-
sive scale without imposing any limits on your capabili-
ties. When you think big, you overestimate what you can
achieve, allowing you to achieve great success and reach
your full potential.

Big thinkers are fearless, bold, optimistic, creative, positive, open-minded, and want to be extraordinary. Small
thinkers underestimate what they can achieve, lower their

expectations, limit themselves, and in turn underestimate their capability and outcomes.

Next, I provide some practical ways to challenge the way you think, stretch your thinking, and create an unstoppable mind.

Believe in Yourself

The power to be whoever you want to be lies within you. If you believe in yourself, other people will start to believe in you. Believe you are in total control of your destiny. Have confidence in your ability to achieve anything with the right knowledge and mentorship.

If confidence does not come naturally to you, cultivate it. One way to cultivate confidence is to keep a journal of your past accomplishments like getting an advanced degree, birthing and raising a child, or planning a big event.

Document your accomplishments to help you visualize your value, believe in your abilities, and increase your confidence to accomplish bigger goals.

Be Creative and Open-Minded

Creativity is the mother of invention. Create new opportunities for yourself and stop waiting for others to invite you. Open your mind to new opportunities by asking yourself challenging questions about how you can use your talents, passion, and skills to solve a problem. Your ability to solve one problem with your talent(s) will create a floodgate of new opportunities.

Visualize new possibilities for your future and allow your imagination to soar and carry you as far as possible without setting any limits with your mind. Explore and identify new ways to turn your imaginations into ideas and your ideas into goals.

Be willing to step out of your comfort zone and be open to change. Be willing to take uncomfortable actions. Allow yourself to see things in different ways and be willing to find new solutions to old problems.

Set Big Goals

If you set big goals, you will achieve big things; likewise, if you set small goals, you will achieve small things. Create aspirational goals that excite you and work toward your big goals in small incremental steps. The size of your belief will ultimately determine the size of your success.

Create a Vision Board and an Achievement Board

Everything starts with a vision. Visualize what you want to achieve and write it down. If you know where you are going, you can create a roadmap to get there. Document your dreams, goals, and desires visibly on a *vision or dream board* in your work space to inspire and motivate you.

Create a separate space on your vision board for your professional and personal goals. Place your most immediate goals at the top of the vision board and your longer-term goals further down. Focus on your immediate goal(s) first.

Move the goals you have achieved from your vision board to your achievement board. Seeing what you are able to achieve will fuel your vision for bigger goals.

Stay Positive and Optimistic

Break down all barriers of self-doubt in your mind and eliminate all negative words that produce small thinking.

Build positive thinking by eliminating all negative words from your vocabulary. Examples of negative words are "I can't do it", "it is impossible", "I am not worthy" and "I am not good enough."

Maintain positivity by speaking words of affirmation to yourself daily. Examples of affirmative words are "I can do anything I set my mind to," "I am great," "I am worthy," and "I am capable of achieving great things."

Start your day with activities that generate positive energy like prayer, meditation, devotion, yoga, exercise, and calming music. Maintain positive energy throughout your day by visibly displaying positive and inspirational quotes in your work space.

Stay optimistic by focusing on the opportunities around you rather than the obstacles. Stay encouraged as cultivating positive thinking takes time, practice, and repetition to turn it into a habit.

Surround Yourself with Doers

You are the company you keep, so surround yourself with believers, positive thinkers, and doers. Find successful people in your areas of interest either in your immediate environment or in an online community.

Connect with people who inspire you and help you believe you can achieve your goals too. Share your ideas with your network to get feedback, and find investors within your network if you need capital to turn your ideas into reality.

It takes big thinking to achieve big results. Do not underestimate the power of big thinking in achieving your life goals. On the next page, I summarize the main take away messages from the principle of "Thinking Big" and I provide some reflection exercises for you to complete.

Next, we will move to the second principle: "Conquer Your Fears".

Whatever you are thinking. Think Bigger.
–Tony Hsien

Think Big Take Away Message

Your mind is your most powerful asset, use your mind to drive your success by thinking big.

Believe in yourself: Believe you are in total control of your destiny and your ability to achieve anything.

Be creative and open minded: Ask challenging questions to open up your mind to solving problems with your talent(s) and let your imagination take you as far as possible.

Set big and aspirational goals that excite you and work toward your big goals in small incremental steps.

Visualize what you want to achieve and document them on a vision board. Create an achievement board to document the goals you have achieved to fuel your vision for bigger goals.

Stay positive and optimistic: Start your day with activities that generate positive energy. Maintain positivity throughout your day by focusing on the opportunities rather than the obstacles.

Surround yourself with big thinkers and doers to motivate you and help you turn your ideas into reality.

Reflection

Write down your three strongest talents.

Is your career aligned with your talents?
If not, identify three new opportunities
or goals that align with your talents.

Write down three practical things you will start
doing right now to think big toward your goal.

Conquer Your Fears

The only thing we have to fear is fear itself
–Franklin D. Roosevelt

What is Fear?

Fear is "an unpleasant and strong emotion often caused by anticipation and awareness of danger."[4] One type of fear is associated with avoiding physical pain such as fear of heights, darkness, death, or creatures like snakes or spiders. This type of fear is inborn, helps you to avoid danger, but is unlikely to impede your success in life. The other type of fear is associated with your identity. Identity fear can cause psychological and emotional pain that paralyzes you. This type of fear can hold you back from implementing your ideas or reaching your full potential.

Identity fear can manifest itself as fear of criticism or fear of rejection. This comes from the fear that others will judge you as not qualified or judge your ideas or work as

---

[4] "Fear," Merriam-Webster (Merriam-Webster, n.d.), accessed 2021, https://www.merriam-webster.com/dictionary/fear.

not good enough. People who have a perfectionist personality tend to suffer from this type of fear. As a perfectionist myself, I know that this fear makes you feel like you are inadequate unless you are perfect, and you believe that others will likely judge you or your work as imperfect too.

There is a saying by Aristotle that "the only way to avoid criticism is to say nothing, do nothing, and be nothing." That about sums it up. If you want to be something, you cannot be afraid of criticism. Successful people are less focused on self-image or what other people think of them but are more focused on learning, acting, and growing.

Identity fear can also manifest as fear of failure or fear of the unknown. When you are afraid to fail or you do not know how to execute an idea, you simply do not try. You continue to use the excuse that you do not know how to reach your goals to hold yourself back. The only difference between the people who succeed and people who do not is that people who succeed actually tried. Even if you fail, you have learned from your mistakes.

Fear is real and it is a part of your success journey. No matter what type of fear you have, you cannot allow it to hold you back. You have to acknowledge the fear in order to move forward.

Next, I provide some practical ways to conquer your fears.

Confront Your Fears and Act in Spite of Fear

First, acknowledge that you are afraid. Keep a journal to document your fears, how fear makes you feel, and how you react when fear arises. Documenting your fears will create awareness, help you identify ways to counteract them, and give you the courage to face them.

Expose yourself to the things or situations where you are afraid to create familiarity and reduce your fear. If you run away from the things or situations where you are afraid, you will never be able to face them.

For example, as an author, you may be afraid to write that new book. Your fear may stem from not knowing how to get started, or feeling that you are not providing new information, or that your book may not sell.

You can counteract each of these fears by taking actions like

- Researching how to write a book,
- Acknowledging that your information may not be new but will be written from your own unique perspective, or
- Sharing your ideas with other authors to get feedback and getting motivated by their success stories.

Commit to Your Success

Achieving big goals is about commitment and not convenience. It is not convenient to commit the time and energy necessary to achieve big goals. It takes commitment, dedication, persistence, and continuous uncomfortable actions to turn your big goals into reality.

Identify what motivates you to embark on your success journey. Your motivation is your "WHY". Ask yourself *why* you want to be successful. Your "WHY" may be achievement, independence, financial freedom, legacy, or improving the well-being of humanity. Whatever motivates you, cling to it and let it fuel your drive to success.

Be Confident in Your Knowledge

Many people feel that they need to know everything about a topic before they can take any action. Do not let great be the enemy of good. Acquire sufficient knowledge in the area of business on which you are embarking—by all means, empower yourself with the right knowledge to avoid common pitfalls.

However, at some point, you must believe in your ability to problem-solve and have confidence that you know enough to take the plunge. You will refine your knowledge over time as you take more action toward your goal.

Focus on the Reward, Not the Obstacles

To achieve your goals, focus on the reward or what you stand to gain rather than the obstacles or what you stand to lose. This will allow you to stay optimistic and positive throughout your success journey.

There will always be obstacles, but do not let them stop you from moving forward toward your goals. Always look beyond the obstacles and see overcoming each obstacle as getting one step closer to your goal.

Focus on the Process, Not the Outcome

Focus on the process and the actions you need to take rather than waiting for the outcome or results to reduce your stress level. Focusing your efforts on your progress will give you the confidence to keep moving forward. Reward yourself with a treat you enjoy every time you take a significant step forward toward your goal.

Find Support, not Approval

Find and connect with like-minded people in your immediate environment or online for extra motivation, but do not wait for the approval of others.

The need for approval and the fear of failure are more of the same and they do not achieve any positive results.

Ensure that your motivation is from within yourself and believe in your ability to achieve your goals without much external approval.

Avoid Unhealthy Competition

To be honest, it takes some level of competitiveness to be an achiever and most successful people have a Type A personality. This type of personality is typically more ambitious, competitive, and aggressive and has high expectations of them self and others. As much as these personality traits can drive achievement, they can also be detrimental if you allow these traits to take over.

No matter how accomplished you are, there will always be someone more accomplished than you. The only person you should compete with is you. Unhealthy competition breeds jealousy, dissatisfaction, and unhappiness.

Stay focused on your own goals to avoid unhealthy competition. See achievement of others as an inspiration to create your own goals rather than a threat.

Be Aware of Your Physical response to Fear

Stop and take a break when you feel any physical signs of fear such as rapid heartbeat, shortness of breath, chest pain, dry mouth, sweating, or trembling.

Counteract your physical response to fear by practicing calming activities like deep breathing, yoga, meditation, listening to calming music, or taking a nature walk. These activities will help calm your body and clear your thoughts so you can refocus your mind on the positive reasons for embarking on your journey.

Do not allow fear to prevent you from exploring new opportunities, setting new goals, or maximizing your full potential. On the next page, I summarize the main take away messages from the principle of "Conquering Your Fears" and I provide some reflection exercises for you to complete.

Next, we will move to the third principle: "Seek and Acquire Knowledge".

Do the things you fear to do and keep on doing it. That is the quickest and surest way ever yet discovered to conquer fear.
–Dale Carnegie

Conquer Your Fears
Take Away Message

Fear can manifest as fear of rejection or fear of failure.

Fear is real. You must acknowledge your fear to move forward.

Confront your fear by documenting them and take actions in spite of fear.

Commit to your success: Identify your "WHY" and let it fuel your drive to success.

Be confident in your knowledge. You do not need to be an expert to embark on your journey. You will learn best by acting.

Focus on what you stand to gain rather than what you stand to lose.

Focus on your progress rather than the outcome to reduce your stress and increase your confidence.

Find and connect with like-minded doers for extra motivation but do not wait for anyone's approval.

Stay focused on your own goals to avoid unhealthy competition. See the achievement of others as inspiration, rather than a threat to your success.

Stay mindful of your physical response to fear. Practice calming activities to counteract any negative physical reaction to fear.

Reflection

Write down three things that terrify you about taking action toward your goals.

Identify your "WHY" for wanting to embark on your journey. Is it doing what you love, financial independence, giving back, or legacy for family? Write down your three big motivations.

Seek and Acquire Knowledge

Life is a school, make a habit of always educating yourself.
–Unknown author

What is Knowledge?

Knowledge includes "facts, information, or skills acquired by a person through education or experience."[5] Knowledge can be theoretical as acquired through education or practical as acquired through experience. For example, a civil engineer is knowledgeable about building infrastructures such as roads and bridges by acquiring a degree in civil engineering (theoretical knowledge), or by practicing in the field of civil engineering (practical knowledge), or both.

Knowledge is power. Seek knowledge in your areas of interest so you can grow in the subject matter. Be resource-

---

[5] "Knowledge: Definition of Knowledge by Oxford Dictionary on Lexico. com Also Meaning of Knowledge," Lexico Dictionaries | English (Lexico.com, 2020), https://www.lexico.com/definition/knowledge.

ful and invest in acquiring new knowledge by reading books, articles, and journals, listening to webinars and podcasts, taking classes, attending seminars, conferences, and trainings in your areas of interest. Acquiring the necessary knowledge will increase your confidence and help you achieve your goal.

Beware of information overload. In this information age, you can be easily overwhelmed just by searching the World Wide Web. Quantity does not always equal quality. The quality of information you consume matters more than the quantity. Focus on acquiring good quality information because the success of your output will depend on the quality of your input.

Next, I provide some practical ways to find and acquire good quality information.

Identify and Prioritize What You Need to Learn

After you have identified your goal, break your goal down into the steps you need to accomplish it. Next, identify the type of information you need to accomplish each step and focus your search on the necessary information.

For example, if your goal is to write a book, you can break the book writing process down into steps like;

- Identify the topic for your book
- Create a mind map and outline for your book
- Write a draft of each chapter of your book
- Find an editor to edit the draft of your book
- Format the final draft of your book
- Design the cover for your book

- Find a publisher or self-publish your book
- Promote your book once it is published

Breaking down the knowledge you need into manageable steps will help you focus your knowledge search and keep you from getting distracted by all the extra information out on the World Wide Web.

Identify and Use Credible Sources

Credible sources provide good quality information. Sources of information like textbooks or journals may be more credible than online blogs. Likewise, paid classes offered by experts may be more credible and useful than free podcasts available online. Invest in yourself and pay for good quality information to move you quickly toward your goal.

You can assess the credibility of your sources by the qualification of the author, the success and reputation of the author, how frequently the author is cited, and the quality of information the author provides.

Good quality information is relevant, accurate, consistent, clear, and current. Time is a limited resource, so find and use credible sources to ensure you are learning the right information and managing your time efficiently.

Focus Your Learning on Specific Knowledge

Now that you know exactly what you need to learn and the best resources to help you learn what you need, focus your time on acquiring the *specific knowledge* you need to accomplish each step of your goal to increase efficiency.

Use a calendar to schedule what you need to learn daily or weekly to keep you on track to achieve your learning goals.

Practice Your Knowledge

Learning is a lifelong process. As you acquire new knowledge, practice using your new knowledge to develop new skills. This is known as active learning and it involves deliberately turning your knowledge into action and repeating the action with the intent of reaching a goal.

Actively practicing your knowledge will increase your confidence and competence and move you toward achieving your goals quickly. Later on, we will discuss more specific strategies for taking action and practicing your knowledge.

On the next page, I summarize the main take away messages from the principle of "Seeking and Acquiring Knowledge" and I provide some reflection exercises for you to complete.

Next, we will move to the fourth principle: "Find Mentors".

To change your output, you need to change your input.
–Unknown Author

Seek and Acquire Knowledge
Take Away Message

Identify and prioritize what you need to learn by breaking down your goal into steps you need to accomplish your goal.

Identify and pay for credible sources that provide good quality information to move you quickly toward your goal.

Focus your learning on the specific knowledge you need to accomplish your goal.

Actively practice using your new knowledge to develop new skills.

Reflection

Break down your most immediate goal into steps and identify the specific knowledge you need for each step of your goal.

Identify and write down two to three credible sources of information you will use to acquire the specific knowledge you need for each step.

Do your regular sources of information, including social media, reflect your goal? If not, write down *one* practical way you will reduce time spent on sources that do not reflect your goals and increase time spent on sources that reflect your goals.

Find Mentors

> One of the greatest values of mentors is the ability
> to see ahead what others cannot see and to help
> them navigate a course to their destination.
> –John C. Maxwell

Who is a Mentor?

A *mentor* is "an experienced person who helps someone with less experience to achieve their goals."[6] A mentor can be someone who has achieved the goals you want to achieve and whose accomplishments inspire you to pursue your dreams.

The role of a mentor can take multiple forms. For example, a mentor can be a role model, a guide, a teacher, an advisor, an advocate, or a motivator at different times in the mentoring relationship.

---

[6] "Mentor," Mentor noun - Definition, pictures, pronunciation and usage notes | Oxford Advanced Learner's Dictionary at OxfordLearnersDictionaries.com (Oxford University Press, n.d.), accessed 2021, https://www.oxfordlearnersdictionaries.com/us/definition/english/mentor.

Here are specific examples of different forms a mentor can take to impact your career, business, or family life.

Role model: A mentor can be a role model by sharing their experience with you. A mentor can share practical examples of how they overcame challenges and achieved their career, business, or family goals.

Guide: A mentor can provide guidance on exploring different career options, setting career goals, starting a new business, developing professional or business contacts, and finding resources to advance your career, build your business, or manage your family and career obligations.

Teacher: A mentor can help you acquire the confidence and competence you need by providing precise knowledge in specific areas of your career, business, or family life.

Advisor: A mentor can be a source of wisdom. A mentor can listen to your challenges and provide feedback, ask difficult questions about your career, business, or family, encourage you to think critically through your challenges, and open your mind to new and different perspectives.

Advocate: A mentor can be an advocate by envisioning the long-range view of your career or business and be willing to support your growth and development by connecting you with career or business opportunities and recommending you to future employers or business partners.

Motivator: A mentor can motivate you by offering encouragement and emotional support. A mentor can be a sounding board for ideas and provide insight into possible opportunities. A mentor can challenge you to succeed and show you how to navigate your challenges by sharing their personal challenges and success stories.

Finding a Mentor

Finding the right mentor can be challenging but not impossible. Do not overlook people in your immediate environment such as your friends, relatives, neighbors, teachers, coworkers, or spiritual leaders. They may possess the knowledge or skill you need, and you already have established relationship with them.

You can also find mentors in other parts of your immediate environment such as your places of worship, volunteer centers, fitness centers, and shopping centers. By engaging and talking to different people in your immediate environment, you can identify people that possess the knowledge and skills you need and are happy to help you.

Many times, you have to look outside of your immediate environment to find mentors. Here are examples of places you can look for mentors outside of your immediate environment.

WorkPlace or Professional Society: Many organizations or professional societies have formal or informal mentorship programs that match mentors to mentees based on the mentee's specific needs or areas of desired growth. Join mentorship programs within your organization or professional societies to find a mentor that fits your professional growth needs.

Industry Events: If you are looking for a mentor in a specific industry, you can look for formal industry events such as trade shows, conferences, networking events, speaking events, or informal meet-ups advertised online, in trade magazines, or in industry newsletters.

Online Mentorship Programs: You can find mentors by joining online mentoring programs that specialize in pairing young professionals with potential mentors. An example of such a program is findamentor.com, an online program where you can sign up and find mentors in your areas of interest.

Social Media: Mentors can be found by searching social media platforms like Twitter, Facebook, Instagram, and professional platforms like LinkedIn. You can use specific criteria on any of these social media platforms to find reputable individuals in the industry of your interest. Follow these experts over time to become more familiar with their work and assess their willingness to engage or talk to others who are new to the industry.

You can also search for online mastermind communities in your field of interest and request to join such groups for free or for a fee. A mastermind community is a group of people connected by similar goals and a desire to grow and make progress in a specific area of interest.

Maximizing Your Mentorship Relationship

As a mentee, you have a significant role in driving the mentor/mentee relationship. Here are examples of ways to successfully engage as a mentee and maximize your mentorship experience.

- Identify the knowledge you want to acquire or the skills you want to build.
- Do your research and talk to potential mentors to find someone who possesses the knowledge or skill you need, values mentorship, is willing to share their time and experience with you, and is a good fit for your personality.
- If it is a formal relationship, set clear rules of engagement upfront by establishing the expectations, responsibilities, mode of communication, and frequency of communication.
- Commit to the learning process by keeping and being on time for all scheduled appointments and actively engage in building the relationship with your mentor to maximize your experience.
- Share your goals and struggles openly with your mentor for an effective mentoring experience.
- Ask specific questions about how best to handle your struggles and be open to hearing feedback.
- Ask for practical examples of how your mentor overcame their challenges and achieved their goals.
- Research, evaluate, and follow-up with every guidance from your mentor and apply the guidance as they fit with your own situation.

- When you have accomplished your goal of the mentoring relationship, communicate your accomplishments to your mentor, and thank them for their time.

The Truth About Mentorship

Do not limit yourself with inaccurate pre-conceived notions about what a mentoring relationship is supposed to be. I used to see mentorship as a formal, long-term relationship with one person at a time, or only with someone of my gender or race. People who think like this are likely to miss out on potential productive mentoring relationships. Keep in mind

- Mentorship does not have to be a formal relationship with scheduled and recurring meetings. It can also be informal casual conversations over time.
- A mentoring relationship can be short- or long-term. Mentors may be for a season depending on your goals, where you are in life, and what you are trying to learn from your mentors. You can also have different mentors for different life goals.
- Mentors do not have to be of the same gender or race as the mentee. Women can benefit from the go-getter mindset of male mentors, while males can benefit from the multi-tasking ability of female mentors. Similarly, people of different races can benefit from the expanded perspectives and life experiences of mentors of a different race.

On the next page, I summarize the main take away messages from the principle of "Finding Mentors" and I provide some reflection exercises for you to complete.

Next, we will move to the last principle: "Act and Follow Through".

Show me a successful individual and I will show you someone who had a real positive influence on his or her life. I don't care what you do for a living—if you do it well, I am sure there was someone cheering you on or showing you the way. A mentor.
–Denzel Washington

Find Mentors Take Away Message

A mentor is an experienced person who helps someone with less experience to achieve their goals.

A mentor can be a role model, a guide, a teacher, an advisor, an advocate, or a motivator at different times during the mentoring relationship.

You can find mentors within and outside of your immediate environment.

Focus on finding mentors that possess the knowledge you need and skills you want to build, values mentorship, are willing to share their time and experience with you, and fits with your personality.

Establish the expectations for the relationship upfront, share your goals and challenges openly, and be open to hearing feedback.

Research, evaluate, and follow-up with each guidance from your mentors and apply each guidance to your situation as it fits.

Commit to the learning process by following through with all mentoring appointments to maximize your mentoring experience.

Reflection

Based on your goals, write down three specific types of knowledge you want to acquire, or skills you want to build.

Write down three qualities you want in a mentor. Look in and outside of your immediate environment to identify potential mentors.

Write down three expectations for your mentoring relationship and three specific actions you will take to commit to the relationship.

Act and Follow Through

> Vision without action is a daydream. Action
> without vision is a nightmare.
> −Japanese Proverb

Act and Follow Through

The only way to get to your next level is to take action and follow-through. Taking *action* is "the process of doing something in order to make something happen, achieve a goal, or to deal with a situation."[7]

Acting and following through is by far, the most important of the five principles laid out in this book, but it is also the most challenging. Without accomplishing the first four principles of "Thinking Big", "Conquering your Fears", "Seeking and Acquiring Knowledge", and "Finding Mentors", it is almost impossible to successfully accomplish

---

[7] "Action," Action noun - Definition, pictures, pronunciation and usage notes | Oxford Advanced American Dictionary at OxfordLearners Dictionaries.com (Oxford University Press), accessed 2021, https://www.oxfordlearnersdictionaries.com/definition/american_english/action.

the last principle of "Acting and Following Through". In fact, the first four principles are the foundation upon which the last principle should be built.

You can practice all four principles and still not take any action toward your goals. Many people get stuck in the fear stage or the knowledge acquisition stage and never take any specific action toward their goals. Unfortunately, life does not reward you for what you know but rather for what you do.

Taking action toward your goal is sometimes uncomfortable, uneasy, and inconvenient. It will take vision, prioritization, commitment, dedication, consistency, and perseverance to achieve your goal.

Next, I provide some specific and practical ways to start taking action toward your goals today.

Write Down Your Goal(s) and Timeline(s)

This may sound too basic but simply writing down your goal(s) with timeline(s) for when you want to accomplish the goal(s) is an important step. Be specific when writing down your goals. For example, write "I want to write and publish a book by March 2021" and not just "I want to be a published author." Writing down your goals with specificity, clarity, and a timeline increases your chances of realizing your goals.

If you have multiple goals, prioritize them in the order of ease of accomplishment, importance, and urgency, and designate them as immediate (e.g. in the next year), mid-term (e.g. in the next three to five years), and long-term goals (e.g. in the next eight to ten or more years).

Break Down Your Goal(s) into a Stepwise Plan

To accomplish any goal, you have to start with a plan, as you cannot execute a plan that you have not made. If you have multiple goals, start with your most immediate goal.

Create a plan for your goal by identifying specific and actionable steps to achieve your goal. Next, break down your goal(s) into the steps you have identified to make it easier to execute. You can identify steps needed to start a project by searching on the internet, asking someone who has done it before, or finding a book that breaks down 'how to accomplish' the task. Assign realistic timelines to each step to keep yourself accountable. Depending on the goal, you can build some reasonable flexibility into your timeline.

For example, if you are a busy mom with young children and a full-time job and you have a goal to start a Masters' in Business Administration (MBA) degree, break down the process for finding, preparing, and applying to the appropriate programs into a step-wise monthly plan with timelines as illustrated in the figure.

Goal: Start an MBA Degree
by January 2022

**Step-wise Plan to Accomplish the Goal
of Starting an MBA. Complete Each Step
by the End of the Assigned Month.**

1. Identify schools offering MBA programs with evening or online classes: January 2021
2. Enroll in GMAT test preparation classes: January 2021
3. Set-up monthly practice exams for GMAT: February 2021
4. Schedule actual GMAT exam: March 2021
5. Request for transcript and letters of recommendation from undergraduate program: April 2021
6. Complete GMAT Exam: May 2021
7. Submit applications to identified graduate programs: June 2021
8. Contact schools to ensure applications are complete for January 2022 admission: July 2021

Take Daily and Consistent
Action Toward Your Goal

Knowing what you need to do and when you need to do it is a *big* step toward achieving your goal. Commit to your plan and execute each step according to your predetermined timeline.

Start at the beginning of your plan and take specific and consistent actionable steps every day towards your goal no matter how small.

Do the steps you are good at first. Find help for the steps you need more expertise to accomplish. Celebrate every step you accomplish towards your goal.

Take on Unplanned Opportunities

Take on good opportunities even if they are not on your list of immediate goals. Accomplishing a goal will likely open up new opportunities you were not expecting. Saying *yes* to new unplanned opportunities will open up even bigger opportunities to reach your potential.

Manage Your Time Wisely

Planning and managing your time will help increase your productivity and reduce your stress level. It is not about how much time you have, it is about how you use the time you have.

Create a routine for your day and start your day early when you are most refreshed to maximize the day.

To avoid procrastination, use a time management tool like a planner or calendar to plan your week and day ahead. Make a list of what you want to accomplish weekly, over the weekend and daily, the night before.

Prioritize your daily to-do list based on urgency and importance. Break big tasks down into smaller tasks and record a realistic timeline to accomplish each smaller task to keep you on track. Be honest with yourself as you plan your weekly and daily deliverables and do not overpromise and underdeliver for yourself. Tackle each task one at a time and check off each task as you accomplish them to help motivate you.

Stay Organized and Avoid Distraction

Have a clean dedicated workspace with minimal to no distractions to work. Dedicate a specific number of hours a day to work on your assigned daily tasks.

Keep your calendar and deadlines visible in your workspace to keep you on track. Avoid distractions like social media, news briefs, personal emails, and phone calls while getting through your daily tasks.

Put your phone on silent, set a Do Not Disturb mode on your phone, or put your phone away during your work hours.

If you have young children and need to be reached during your work hours, check your calls or text messages intermittently when you take your breaks.

Social media could be a big distraction and time-waster. Unless you are using social media to promote your business, set a daily limit for how much time you spend on social media.

Stay Connected to The Right Network

Stay connected to your mentors, partners, and/or network of like-minded people within your immediate environment, professional societies, and/or mastermind communities.

Like-minded people will value your ideas, appreciate your journey, open your mind to new possibilities, encourage you, and keep you accountable along your journey. This is an important aspect of your success journey.

The lesson is not just in succeeding but in taking consistent actionable steps toward your goal(s). Even if you do not succeed the first time, you have learned something from the actions you have taken, and you will be more prepared to succeed the next time.

Fear of failure is real, and it may creep up from time to time along your success journey. Use all five principles, stay focused, positive, and connected to the right network of people for the extra motivation you need to keep moving toward your goal(s).

On the next page, I summarize the main take away messages from the principle of "Acting and Following Through" and I provide some reflection exercises for you to complete.

A journey of a million miles begins with one step.
–Chinese proverb

Act and Follow Through
Take Away Message

Acting is the most important principle for achieving success.

Document your goals, create a plan with actionable steps and realistic timelines.

Take specific and consistent action toward your goal everyday no matter how small.

Take on good opportunities, even if they are unplanned to open up even bigger opportunities to reach your potential.

Manage your time wisely, stay organized, and remove all sources of distraction during your work hours.

Stay connected to a network of like-minded people for extra motivation.

Reflection

Make a list of your short-term, mid-term, and long-term goals.

Look over your short-term goals. Pick one goal for this year. Break down the goal into small and specific actionable steps with defined timelines.

Write down three strategies you will use to stay focused on taking daily action toward your goal.

Find Your Purpose, Change Your Mindset, and Fulfill Your Potential

In the last section, we discussed identifying your talents and changing your mindset to fulfill your potential through five main principles. The principles of "Thinking Big", "Conquering Your Fears", "Seeking and Acquiring Knowledge", "Finding Mentors", and "Acting and Following Through" are important for driving and achieving your goals. I also provided specific ways to actualize each of these five principles as summarized below.

Think Big

- **Believe in Yourself:** Have confidence in your ability to achieve anything with the right knowledge and mentorship.
- **Be Creative and Open-Minded:** Open up your mind to identify new opportunities. Ask challenging questions to solve problems with your talent(s) and let your imagination take you as far as possible.

Identify ways to turn the opportunities into ideas and the ideas into goals.

- **Set Big Goals:** Create aspirational goals that excite you and work toward your big goals in small incremental steps.
- **Create a Vision Board and an Achievement Board:** Visualize what you want to achieve and write it down to inspire and motivate you. Create an achievement board to document the goals you have achieved to fuel your vision for bigger goals.
- **Be Positive and Optimistic:** Build positive thinking by eliminating all self-doubt. Stay optimistic by focusing on the opportunities and rewards and not the obstacles and challenges.
- **Surround Yourself with Doers:** Surround yourself with believers, positive thinkers, and doers to keep you motivated along your success journey.

Conquer Your Fears

- **Confront Your Fears and Act in Spite of Fear**: Acknowledge your fear, document your fear to create awareness, and counteract your fear by taking action.
- **Commit to Your Success**: Identify your "WHY" for your journey and let your motivation fuel your drive to success. It takes commitment, dedication, persistence, and continuous action to turn your goals into reality.
- **Be Confident in Your Knowledge:** Acquire sufficient knowledge in your area of interest, and be

confident you know enough to take action. You will refine your knowledge over time as you take more action.

- **Focus on the Reward:** Focus on what you stand to gain rather than what you stand to lose. Focus on the reward rather than the obstacles. See overcoming obstacles as being a step closer to your goal.

- **Focus on the Process**: Focus on your progress rather than the outcome. Focusing on your progress will reduce your stress, increase your confidence, and keep you moving toward your goals.

- **Find Support, not Approval:** Find and connect with like-minded people in your immediate or external environment for extra motivation, but do not wait for the approval of others.

- **Avoid Unhealthy Competition:** Stay focused on your own goals to avoid unhealthy competition. See the achievement of others as inspiration, rather than a threat to your success.

- **Be Aware of Your Physical Response:** Counteract your physical response to fear by practicing calming activities like deep breathing, meditation, or nature walks.

Seek and Acquire Knowledge

- **Identify and Prioritize Your learning:** Identify and break down the knowledge you need to accomplish your goal(s) into manageable steps. This will help focus your knowledge search and avoid distractions.

- **Identify and Use Credible Sources:** Find credible sources to ensure you are learning the right information and managing your time efficiently. Assess source credibility by checking the qualification and reputation of the author and the quality of the information.
- **Focus on Specific Knowledge**: Focus your time on acquiring the *specific knowledge* you need to accomplish each step of your goal to increase efficiency. Use a calendar to schedule what you need to learn daily or weekly to keep you on track to achieving your learning goals.
- **Practice Your Knowledge:** Actively turn your knowledge into actions to develop new skills. Practicing your knowledge will increase your confidence and competence and move you toward your goals quickly.

Find Mentors

- **Identify a Mentor:** A mentor is an experienced person who helps someone with less experience achieve their goals. A mentor can be a role model, a guide, a teacher, an advisor, an advocate, or a motivator at different times in the mentoring relationship.
- **Find a Mentor:** You can find mentors in your immediate environment such as your friends, family, or community circle or outside of your immediate environment such as in professional networks and online mentoring programs. Find a mentor who possesses the knowledge you need or skill you want to acquire, values mentorship, and is willing to share their time and experience with you.

- **Maximize the Mentoring Relationship:** Keep and be on time for all scheduled appointments. Actively engage in driving and building the relationship by being open with your struggles, asking practical questions, and following up with each guidance to maximize your mentoring experience.

Act and Follow Through

- **Write Down Your Goal(s) and Timeline(s):** Write down your specific goals and identify the timeline for each goal. Prioritize your goals and start with your immediate or short-term goals. Build some flexibility into your plan to take on unplanned good opportunities.
- **Break Your Goals Down into a Step-Wise Plan:** Create a plan for your goals by identifying specific and actionable steps you need to achieve each goal. Assign realistic timelines to each step of your plan.
- **Take Daily and Consistent Actions Toward Your Goal:** Commit to your plan and execute each step of your plan according to your predetermined timeline. Take daily and consistent action toward your plan no matter how small. Celebrate every step you accomplish toward your goal.
- **Take on Unplanned Opportunities:** Say yes to good unplanned opportunities to open up even bigger opportunities for reaching your potential.
- **Manage Your Time Wisely:** Plan your week and day ahead and create a routine for your day to avoid

procrastination, increase productivity, and reduce your stress level.

- **Stay Organized and Avoid Distraction:** Create a dedicated workspace. Keep your calendar and deadlines visible in your workspace. Dedicate a specific number of hours a day to work on your goals and avoid distractions during your work hours.
- **Stay Connected to the Right Network:** Stay connected to your network of like-minded people for extra motivation.

Practice these five principles for any goal you have to achieve success. Think big when identifying your goals, conquer your fears by facing them, seek and acquire the right knowledge and skills, find mentors to guide you along the way, and take daily and consistent action toward your goals. Practicing these principles will increase your confidence and competence, and will successfully move you toward achieving your life goals.

> If you can imagine it, you can achieve it. If
> you can dream it, you can become it.
> –William Arthur War

Applying The Five Principles to Your Everyday Life

You cannot go back and change the beginning, but you
can start where you are and change the ending.
–C.S. Lewis

In this section, I evaluate different aspects of a woman's life as a professional or entrepreneur, mother, and wife to further expand on ways you can apply these principles to the different aspects of your life.

The role of a woman is complex. Your role as a professional or entrepreneur and your role as a wife and mother can sometimes be at conflict. Climbing the corporate ladder or starting a new business can be even more challenging if you are raising young children or taking care of a family making the odds of succeeding lower for women. Women have to learn to balance their professional goals with their family obligations, and most successful women will tell you that the struggle is real. Many women have had to sacrifice their career for their desire for a successful marriage and motherhood. Women who have successfully mastered the art of balancing career with family obligations sometimes feel guilty for not being home enough with their children, and this guilt is even more apparent for single mothers with a career.

Every woman's family situation is different. Some women have spouses with demanding jobs who are not able to equally share the family responsibilities. Some women have spouses with less demanding jobs, or who work from home, or work part-time, and are more able to help at home. Some women are single or divorced and do not have a partner to share the family responsibilities. Whatever your family situation, every woman has to find the right balance for herself and her family.

Despite the work/family dilemma, women can succeed in their career while raising a family. Women may have to make some trade-offs initially when their children are younger and need more attention and guidance. It may get easier to balance career and family as children get older and become more self-sufficient. Be honest with yourself in evaluating your family situation. Work smarter, be efficient with your time, set personal limits, and seek family support to find the right balance for your family. Do not be discouraged because each of your goals still can be accomplished using the same set of principles of "Thinking Big", "Conquering Your Fears", "Finding Mentors", "Seeking Knowledge", and "Acting and Following Through"—although the pace at which you achieve your goals may be different during different phases of your life.

The extent to which you need to master each principle may also depend on your talents, personality, and current skills. For example, if you are a naturally logical, systematic, and organized person, but you are introverted, the principles of "Thinking Big", "Conquering Your Fears", and "Finding Mentors", may be more necessary to master than the "Principles of Seeking and Acquiring Knowledge" and "Acting and Following Through". On the other hand, if you are a naturally confident, fearless, extroverted, but disorganized person, the principles of "Seeking and Acquiring Knowledge" and "Acting and Following Through" may be more necessary for you to master than "Thinking Big", "Conquering Your Fears", and "Finding Mentors" as these may come to you more naturally. Although the amount of energy needed to master each principle may vary from person to person based on talents, skills, and personality, all five principles are essential for achieving success.

As you evaluate your different goals as a professional, entrepreneur, wife, and/or mother, it is essential to personalize these principles and match them to your natural abilities and areas of greatest need. My biggest challenges were thinking big and facing my fears. As soon as I was able to master these first two principles, the other three principles of seeking and acquiring knowledge, finding mentors, and acting and following through were much easier for me. As you practice these five principles, you will develop a system and get better at them. Over time, these principles will become your habits and empower you to achieve your goals and maximize your potential.

I will start each part of the next section of this book with lessons from my personal journey to demonstrate how I have applied these principles to my personal goals. Then I will provide additional practical ways to apply the five principles to achieving your goals in the different areas of your life.

This next section is not written in any particular order of importance. Focus on the areas that apply to your situation. For example, if you are a professional woman, who is married and raising young children, then most of the sections may apply to you. But if you are a single professional woman or entrepreneur with no children, then only some of the sections may apply to you. No matter who you are, and what your situation is, there are many practical lessons and practices for everyone to grasp in this next section.

> Habits are the invisible architecture of everyday life.
> –Gretchen Rubin

Applying The Five Principles to Your Professional Journey

> Continuous learning is the minimum
> requirement for success in any field.
> –Dennis Waitley

Lessons from my Professional Journey

When I turned thirteen, my father started a job at an international organization in Abidjan, Ivory Coast, a French speaking beautiful country on the west coast of Africa. My family relocated from Nigeria to the Ivory Coast, but I stayed back in a boarding school in Nigeria since I only had two more years to complete high school. Although I began my formal education in Nigeria, I had the opportunity to complete my advanced high school education outside of Africa in the United Kingdom and my undergraduate and graduate degrees in the United States. Living and schooling in multiple countries as an international student and having to always adjust to new environments and cultures built resilience and persistence in me.

After high school, I completed my undergraduate degree in microbiology, my master's degree in epidemiology and biostatistics, and worked in different research and public health capacities for five years after my master's degree. Although I loved my job as a master's level epidemiologist working in HIV research with an opportunity to give back to my home country Nigeria during the HIV pandemic, I soon realized that I needed a higher degree to make a bigger impact in my field. After thinking through all the educational options available to me and considering my family situation, I decided to pursue a doctoral degree in epidemiology.

After making my decision, I made it my goal to get into an all-expense paid doctoral program the following year. This was important to me as I had completed both my undergraduate and master's degrees debt free, thanks to my wonderful parents who financed my education. Also, 40 percent of Ph.D. students graduate with an average debt of $37,000,[8] so I created a plan to research and apply to multiple doctoral programs where I could combine both my microbiology and epidemiology educational background and receive a full tuition scholarship. I followed my plan and the following year, I was accepted into a full time Molecular Epidemiology program at the University of Maryland with all tuition paid and a stipend for the duration of my five-year program.

When I started my doctoral program, I had no idea what challenges lay ahead but I was committed to my goal.

---

[8] "What Percentage of Americans Have a PhD?," Reference.com (Ask Media Group, LLC, April 8, 2020), https://www.reference.com/world-view/percentage-americans-phd-

I spent the first two years of my program taking full-time classes and a comprehensive exam. I knew I wanted to study infectious diseases, so in the third year of my program, I rotated through three laboratories studying pathogens that cause diseases like malaria and diarrhea with the goal of finding a doctoral mentor in infectious disease. Unfortunately, my goal of finding a mentor was not successful after all three rotations mostly because the mentors could not dedicate the time needed to help me identify a doctoral research topic that was of interest to me. I felt defeated knowing I was running out of time to find a doctoral mentor. Then I remembered a professor who had made an impression on me in my first year because of his passion for teaching. I reached out to him and fortunately, he was willing to accept a new doctoral student. Through this opportunity, I had the good fortune of witnessing his passion for teaching, research, and mentoring first hand. Through this experience, I learned that finding a good mentor is not easy, but focusing on the qualities you desire in a mentor will eventually lead you to the right mentor.

While training on his team for two years, I set another goal to get published during my doctoral training. This was important to me because up until then, I had not been invited to a single scientific publication even though I had worked in research for five years. I informed my mentor of my publication goal and my willingness to get involved in side research projects while completing my doctoral training. Aware of my publication goal, my mentor invited me to participate in many side projects that led to multiple scientific publications that have now been cited by scientists around the world in over a hundred publications.

After five long years of continuous hard work, dedication, and persistence, I received a Ph.D. in Molecular Epidemiology joining about 1.1 percent of the world and 2 percent of adults in the United States between twenty-five and sixty-four years old with a Ph.D. degree,[9] Although my journey to obtain my doctoral degree was challenging, exhausting, and at times frustrating with many sleepless nights and doubtful moments, I stayed focused on my goal and the value that a doctoral degree would add to my life. One such challenging time was in 2008 during the great recession. I was in the third year of my doctoral program, we just bought our second home, and had put all our savings into the home as down payment, then my husband lost his job. With our daughter in daycare, no savings, and no income for five months, we struggled financially, and I seriously contemplated quitting my program to find a job. Thankfully, with great family support and incredible mentors who guided, advised, and advocated for me during my training, we persevered through our financial challenge and my husband found a new job. Sometimes it takes a village of family, friends, and mentors to keep you moving to your next level, so lean on your village as needed.

Fast forward ten years later, as a research scientist and a public health professional at a prestigious United States Federal Agency, I continue to use the same five principles to achieve my professional goals. I have had to stretch my imagination to create a vision for my career. As a scientist

---

9   Alice Clubbs Coldron, "How Rare (or Common) Is It to Have a PhD?," www.FindAPhD.com (FindAUniversity Ltd., December 17, 2019), https://www.findaphd.com/advice/blog/5403/how-rare-or-common-is-it-to-have-a-phd.

from a minority racial group, I still face the fear of being perceived as not being good enough and feeling like I have to prove myself more than my peers. Sometimes I feel like I should be grateful to be given a seat at the scientific research table rather than claiming the seat I have worked hard to earn. At times, when I switched teams, I faced the fear of being perceived as not knowing enough, especially as the new member of the team working with colleagues who have been practicing in the same therapeutic area for decades.

Although these fears are real and may be justified, they limit what you can achieve and how far you can advance professionally. I am determined not to let these fears hold be back. I have faced these fears by taking specific actions like training across teams, volunteering for special projects, stretching beyond my assigned responsibilities, and taking on leadership opportunities to grow my expertise. I actively seek and take on new growth opportunities. I make my interests and goals known to my leadership, so they think of me when new opportunities arise. I seek out new mentors and stay highly engaged inside and outside of my team.

One notable mentorship experience was at my first job after my doctoral training. It was a policy analyst position in pandemic preparedness and response in Washington DC, and I was not immediately clear how I would apply my epidemiology and research training in the policy position. Through talking to my colleagues and supervisors, I found two male mentors who took me under their wings and nurtured my research interests, leading to five scientific publications in my two years as a policy analyst. This experience further solidified in me the importance of finding the right mentors. A few years later, in a different Federal agency and position, I got involved in a mentoring program. When this opportunity presented itself, I was initially hesitant to get involved because I did not feel I had a lot to offer as a mentor, but I signed up for the program anyway. This program now allows me to mentor other professionals and give back while also being mentored.

Many times, I have taken up opportunities that were not on my immediate list of goals because the opportunities presented themselves unexpectedly. One such example was when I took up the opportunity to lead my team for four months, even though, I was the newest member of the team. Unexpected opportunities has taught me to be flexible within my plan, to *say yes* to unplanned opportunities, and not overthink or dismiss them as these are sometimes the best opportunities to learn and grow.

By practicing all five principles of "Thinking Big", "Conquering My Fears", "Finding Mentors", "Seeking Knowledge", and "Acting and Following Through" on my professional journey, I experienced countless opportunities, immense growth, and received several accolades in my career doing what I love to do while serving my country in a public health capacity.

As a growing professional and a mother of three school age kids, there are sometimes conflicts between taking on new professional opportunities and managing my family obligations. I navigated these conflicts by assessing the impact of each professional opportunity on my career and family life. When I took on new professional opportunities, I needed to lean heavily on my family support to meet some of my family obligations during these times. This also allowed me to learn to manage my time more efficiently using practices discussed earlier in this book to ensure that the time I dedicate to my professional responsibilities has minimal impact on the time I spend with my family, especially my children.

Next, I provide some practical ways to use the five principles to maximize your professional journey.

Think Big in Setting Your Professional Goals

Believe in yourself and take charge of your professional destiny. Envision your professional future and set big professional goals. Be bold in your professional pursuits and do not indulge in self-limiting beliefs. Be willing to take professional risks by aiming high. Be creative in finding new growth opportunities. If the opportunities you need to achieve your professional goals do not exist in your immediate environment, create the opportunity for yourself, or look outside of your immediate environment for new opportunities.

Conquer Your Professional Fears

Acknowledge your professional fears and act in spite of your fears. Face your fears by committing to your professional future. Step out of your comfort zone and stretch beyond your assigned responsibilities to grow your expertise quickly. Have confidence in your level of knowledge and do not wait to become an expert to take on new professional roles. Take on unexpected opportunities even if they are not on your list of immediate goals. Focus on the positive impact each professional opportunity will have on your future career. Focus on your own growth opportunities and not what others are doing to avoid distraction or unhealthy competition. Seek support from your superiors but do not ask for permission or approval to pursue new professional opportunities.

Seek and Acquire Professional Knowledge

Seek to understand your organization's structure and culture. Identify the type of training you need to accomplish your professional goals. Continuously identify new growth opportunities inside and outside your organization. Inform your leadership of your professional interests and areas of desired growth, so they think of you when the opportunities arise. Focus on the areas where you need to grow immediately. Train across teams to develop multiple skills.

Find Professional Mentors

Find people who are doing what you want to do professionally and ask them to mentor you. Find and engage mentors inside and outside of your organization who can help you identify new opportunities that align with your professional interests and goals. Join your professional society to find mentors who are willing to share their time and show you how they achieved their professional goals. Maximize all mentoring relationships by following-through with your mentor recommendations.

Act and Follow Through with Your Professional Goals

Document your professional goals and break them down into short- and long-term goals. Start with your short-term professional goal(s) and take small and consistent actionable steps toward your goal(s). For example, if your goal is to get promoted, identify the requirements of the promotion and take the steps needed to fulfill these requirements. These steps can be in the form of taking leadership classes, training across teams, or taking on special projects.

Practice all five principles to pursue your professional ambition to the maximum extent possible.

Be wise in the way you act. Make the most of every opportunity
–Apostle Paul

Professional Journey
Take Away Message

Think big in envisioning your professional future and set big professional goals.

Conquer your fears by taking on new opportunities to achieve your professional goals.

Seek the right knowledge by understanding your organization's structure and culture to identify trainings and growth opportunities.

Find mentors by seeking and finding people who are doing what you want to do professionally and ask them to mentor you.

Document your goals and take small and consistent actionable steps toward your professional goals.

Reflections

Write down your short-term, mid-term, and long-term professional goals.

Start with one short-term goal and create a step-wise plan for your goal with reasonable timeline for each step within your plan.

Write down actionable steps you will take immediately to start working on your chosen short-term professional goal.

Applying The Five Principles to Your Motherhood Journey

Motherhood is amazing. And then it is really hard. And
then it is incredible. And then it is everything in between.
So, hold on to the good, breathe through the bad, and
welcome the wildest and most wonderful ride of your life.
–Proud Happy Mama

Lessons from my Motherhood Journey

Being a mother is the most challenging job in the world.
Unfortunately, there is no playbook for how to be a perfect
mom, and we women navigate motherhood to the best of
our ability. In my thirteen years of being a mother, I have
learned that each child has unique talents, and a mother's
role is to build the whole child physically, emotionally,
mentally, intellectually, and spiritually.

Although I am not a perfect mom, I hold myself to
extremely high esteem in motherhood. I believe empowerment begins at birth, so my long-term motherhood goal
is to empower my children by raising confident, competent, resilient, healthy, and happy children—and eventually

adults. At the beginning of every year, I write and break down my big motherhood goal for the year into specific and tangible goals. These goals may be physical, emotional, mental, social, intellectual, or any combination of these.

Examples of my past motherhood goals include practicing more patience with my children, using more affirmative language with my children, identifying community service opportunities for my children, and helping my children learn instruments in which they are interested. For each of my motherhood goals, I identify a plan of action with an accompanying timeline. For example, my goal of using more affirmative language was to commit to saying three affirmative words to each child daily. So, every day I use words like "you did a great job," "I am proud of you," "you can do it," and "I love you" to meet this specific goal. Over time, this language has become more natural to me, even when I am tired and feeling overwhelmed or frustrated with my children. These affirmative words show my children that their efforts count, and it builds their self-confidence.

One aspect of motherhood that I am learning is identifying and growing each child's unique talents. I am learning that it is better to enroll each child in specific activities focused on growing their individual talents, rather than a variety of different activities that lack focus and may not be interesting to them. Although a variety of activities can help improve their social skills, enhancing their natural abilities will help them excel and build their self-confidence in their talent area. Our first daughter, Dara is a creative and an intellectual. She showed strong interest in academics, arts, and music from a young age. We enrolled her in extra Math and English classes, violin lessons, drawing and painting lessons, and drama camps to grow her intellect and creative skills. She has participated in our county's elementary school honors chorus, her middle school orchestra and middle school drama club, and she has been a member of our church's children and teenage choir for several years. These activities have expanded her intellect, creative talents, and increased her self-confidence as most of these activities involve performing on stage in front of an audience. For high school, she got accepted into a magnet program in a highly ranked public high school in our state and nationally, putting her on an incredible path to academic success and future career and making me a proud mama.

Another aspect of building my children's self-confidence is identifying their areas of weakness and greatest needs and finding the knowledge or services to help strengthen these areas of their lives. When our son, Timi was two years old, we realized that he was not speaking. We decided to seek help from his pediatrician, who referred us to a developmental pediatrician and a behavioral physiologist. We went through a battery of tests, and he was diagnosed with mild autism spectrum disorder. Upon getting his diagnosis, I experienced a flurry of emotions including the fear that my son may never speak. Although it was difficult to comprehend at first and I was afraid, I conquered my fears by researching autism, speaking to other mothers with autistic children, seeking advice from my son's healthcare providers, and finding the right resources to get him on the best path to success. We enrolled our son in our county's early childhood intervention program and a private Adaptive Behavioral Analysis (ABA) program that included speech therapy. He went through two years of intensive early intervention, ABA, and speech therapy programs for five hours a day, five days a week. These programs were highly effective in helping our son overcome his speech challenge. He has been discharged from all three programs and is now talking more than a parrot.

Although our son continues to need help in the areas of attention, focus, and self-direction, he has grown in leaps and bounds. He is now on par with his peers in his academics and well on his way to educational success. I continue to work with his school psychologist and classroom teachers to identify his areas of need and find ways he can be supported in the classroom to continue to build his confidence and competence. His success is a testament to my active role as a mother in seeking the right knowledge, finding the right help, and advocating for my son.

I have also learned it takes a village to raise children. It is important to ask for help when you need it and lean on your support system to help you achieve your motherhood goals. During my Ph.D. training, I leaned heavily on my husband to support our family financially and on my mother for assistance with child care. After I had my first daughter, my mother came to live with us for a year to help care for my daughter while I went through the second year of my program and my comprehensive exams. During those times of juggling first time motherhood with a full-time student load, my mother was my rock. She assisted with bathing, feeding, changing, and nurturing my daughter when I was away in class, studying for an exam, or finishing a term paper. Throughout my children's early childhood years, I learned to ask for childcare help from grandparents and paid babysitters.

I know having grandparents around may not be practical for most families in the Western culture, however, hiring a babysitter for a few hours a day through your neighborhood websites or childcare sites like "care.com" or "sitter-city.com" can go a long way to manage your stress level and balance your motherhood responsibilities. If this type of help is out of reach financially, lean on your spouse and other relatives like a sister, niece, or friend to babysit for a couple of hours from time-to-time to give you a break. I have also outsourced other household responsibilities like housekeeping and laundry as needed to manage my stress level. I find delegating and outsourcing time-consuming household chores helps me focus on other important motherhood tasks like helping my children with their homework and getting them to their extra-curricular activities.

Another aspect of motherhood I am still learning is how to raise children in a blended culture. This happens when families are raising children in a culture different from the culture in which the mother or father were raised. In my situation, both my husband and I are of African descent and we both come from traditional African families with strong cultural norms—like specific ways of greeting and speaking to adults as a sign of respect and a more authoritarian style of parenting. Aspects of this traditional African culture are sometimes in conflict with Western culture in which children are encouraged to speak up, ask questions, and have a voice. I find it challenging to navigate how much of my traditional African culture and how much of the new Western culture to adopt into my parenting style. For example, our middle child, Jola is an embodiment of confidence. From an early age of 8, she already declared she will be studying law at Harvard University. She is determined, assertive, and inquisitive. She challenges everything she is told and asks questions to understand the thinking behind instructions given to her. In my traditional African culture, her confidence to speak up may come across as rude, and I sometimes struggle with how best to constructively manage her assertiveness and inquisitiveness without killing her confident spirit. I manage this by focusing on my role as her mother to correct her language and tone when inappropriate and build on her confidence and determination to achieve her goals.

I also struggle with how to teach my children my native language while living in a predominantly English speaking country, whether or not to allow sleepovers and at what age, and how to balance advising our children to pursue traditional careers (like medicine, law, and engineering) that are highly favored in my traditional African culture versus non-traditional careers (like arts and music) or perhaps find a way to merge both interests successfully. I seek mentor moms who have successfully raised adult children in similar blended-culture situations as mine to help me navigate some of these challenges. One such mentor mom who offers practical and useful advice can be found through her YouTube channel "Optimum Families."

My biggest lesson of all is that motherhood is a journey for which there is no script. We do not have to be perfect as long as we show up for our children with love. As mothers, sometimes we are tired, we forget things, and we even lose our cool, but the most important thing to our children is that our love for them is unconditional and we will do anything to be the best mama to them.

Next, I provide some practical ways to use the five principles to empower your children and maximize your mom potential.

Think Big in Setting Your Motherhood Goals

Think big when setting your motherhood goals. Envision what type of mother you want to be and believe in your ability to be that mother. Identify and write down specific qualities you desire as a mother like loving, strong, supportive, exceptional, and exemplary.

Envision what type of children you want to raise. Identify and write down specific qualities you desire in your children like appreciative, confident, competent, happy, healthy, hardworking, honorable, giving, loving, responsible, respectful, resilient, selfless, and successful.

Believe in your children by setting aspirational goals for them. Identify and grow their individual talents to increase their self-confidence. When they see that you believe in them, they will also start to believe in themselves.

Conquer Your Motherhood Fears

Motherhood is about acting in spite of your fears. This is especially important for first time mothers. Identify what motivates you to create your motherhood goals. Your motivation may be that you want to be the best mother you can be, or you want to raise confident, responsible, and happy adults. Focus on the motivations behind your goals to keep you going when motherhood gets tough.

The outcome of many motherhood goals is long-term, so focus on the progress you are making with your children to keep you going. Sometimes, it may feel like you are saying the same things a thousand times. Even though this can be frustrating, you know your children hear you when they repeat what you are teaching them back to you. An example is when our daughter, Jola tells me not to give up on a goal and tells me she learned it from me. Reward your children when they demonstrate progress, and exhibit positive behavior to motivate them and keep them going.

Connect with like-minded mothers in your immediate environment for resources and support, but do not compare yourself or your children to others. Avoid unhealthy competition with other moms by focusing on your own motherhood goals and believing in the uniqueness of your children.

Seek and Acquire Motherhood Knowledge

Motherhood is about continuous learning. Identify and find the knowledge you need to help your children achieve their goals. The knowledge may be in the areas of growing their talents and/or strengthening their weaknesses. Focus on finding good quality and specific information to help your children achieve their goals.

Find Mentors Moms

For most mothers, their first mentor is their own mother. Tap into the most important motherhood resource in your life—your mother. Fall back on your values and emulate the positive things in your upbringing to the greatest extent possible in raising your own children.

Due to generational differences and evolution of tech-
nology, some things in your upbringing may be more challenging to apply today, so look into your extended family,
friends, neighbors, and religious community for mentor
moms who are successfully raising balanced teenage and
adult children. Engage with these mentor moms to learn
about their experience, seek advice on specific parental
challenges, and obtain referrals for babysitting and extra-
curricular activities.

Be cognizant that no two families are created equal, so
wisely evaluate all information you receive to see how it fits
into your own family life.

Act and Follow Through with Your Motherhood Goals

Document your motherhood goals and identify specific and
tangible steps you can take to achieve your goals. Here are
some practical ways to achieve some specific and common
motherhood goals.

Build Confident Children by Building Their Self-Esteem

Build your child's self-esteem and self-worth by acknowledging their uniqueness and ability to accomplish anything in
which they set their mind. Build your child's self-esteem by:

- Complimenting your children regularly. Always use
  positive language and phrases of affirmation like
  "great job," "you can do it," "never give up," "you are
  the best," "I believe in you," "keep reaching for your

goals," "make the best of every situation," "you are a great asset to the team," and "I love you." Repeating these phrases to your children will go a long way in building their confidence and self-esteem.

- Eliminating derogatory language. Eliminate phrases like "you cannot do it," "you are not good enough," "you are lazy," "everybody is better than you," and similar derogatory language from your daily inter-actions with your children.

- Spending quality time with your children. Create a special bond with each child by finding something special to do with each child. Show your children lots of love with plenty of hugs, kisses, and laugh-ter. The more quality time you spend with your children, the more you will see their unique talents emerge and you can help build their talents and self-confidence.

Build Competent Children by Growing Their Unique Talents

Nurture your children's unique talents to build their pas-sion and encourage them to follow their dreams. Here are some practical ways to grow your children's natural abilities. These gifts are not mutually exclusive, and a child can have multiple gifts.

- For the creative children (singers, songwriters, actors, instrumentalists, writers, designers, or cooks), enroll them in extracurricular activities to perfect their skills and identify a platform to help them practice and gain visibility. For singers, enlist them in a choir.

For songwriters, inspire them to write and record their own music. For writers, guide them to write and publish their stories. Growing children's natural talents will help them blossom and build their confidence.

- For the active children (athletes, gymnasts, swimmers, or runners), engage them in different sports early to identify the sport for which they are a natural fit. Help them join a league or team to increase their skill and gain visibility.

- For the intellectual children (public speakers, high achievers, young scholars), engage them in extra academic activities through free online classes like Khan Academy or paid classes like Kumon, Best Brains, Mathnasium, Code Ninjas, or get a private tutor. Encourage your children to apply to gifted and talented or STEM programs and take advanced placement and honors classes for which they can get college credits while in high school. You can also enroll them in public speaking or debate classes to help increase their confidence and academic excellence.

- For the natural leaders, enroll them in leadership-building camps and find them youth mentor leaders. Although, leaders are born, they can also be made. You can also grow leadership skills in your children on your own by assigning them tasks at home and holding them accountable for their assigned tasks.

- For the budding entrepreneurs, enroll them in entrepreneur camps to teach them about making money, managing money, and multiplying money early in life.

Build Resilient Children by Teaching Self-Care

Life can be challenging and tough, so it is important to raise resilient children who can withstand life's challenges. Here are some practical ways to build resilience in your children:

- Physical self-care: Physical self-care involves eating well-balanced meals, exercising daily, and getting enough sleep to maintain alertness and energy during the day. Have a list of easy-to-make nutritious meals written out and posted on the kitchen refrigerator to ease the meal time burden. Enroll your children in sports or engage them in physical activities like walking, biking, or hiking daily to build physical stamina. Have your children sleep and wake up at set times to get enough sleep and maintain alertness and energy during the day. Teach your children that hard work is important, but taking breaks, resting, and rejuvenating is equally as important.
- Emotional self-care: Emotional self-care involves the ability to problem solve. Help your children build emotional resilience by developing their problem-solving skills. Do not solve every problem for your child but provide the necessary guidance. You can also build emotional resilience by sharing stories about challenging situations you or your children have experienced, and how each of you persevered through and became stronger. For children, chal-

lenges may be in the form of a difficult subject at school, preparing for a test, or a bullying experience. For every difficult situation, ask your child what they will do to solve the problem and teach them how to cope with the negative feelings by finding the positive in the situation.

- Mental self-care: You can build your children's mental resilience by teaching good habits like developing routines, creating task lists for their day, and managing their time. This allows your children to develop a sense of control and the ability to understand that planning and completing tasks fosters a sense of accomplishment and builds mental strength.

- Social self-care: Social resilience starts at home. Ensure that your home is a safe social zone for your children. Make sure your children know their family is their biggest support system. Children who feel safe at home are better equipped to build healthy friendships outside of the home. Help them build safe and healthy social networks by engaging them in extra-curricular activities outside of the home. Ensure your children understand that they bring a unique perspective into every social circle in which they are a part. Teach your children not to copy or compare themselves to other children, but to show leadership and good behavior.

- Spiritual self-care: Build spiritual self-care by providing a strong spiritual foundation for your children. Build spiritual foundation by teaching your children about your religion, and how to pray and trust God. You can also build spiritual foundation by engaging your children in activities in your place of worship, enrolling them in religious education, or enrolling them in religious based schools for their formal education. Children who know they have a creator in whose presence they feel safe and to whom they can express their needs will continue to use this as a source of strength when navigating life's challenges.

- Financial self-care: Teach your children about money from a young age. Start by rewarding them for chores around the house to allow them to earn money and teach the value of work. Teach them to put some of their money away as savings to invest in the future. Get a piggy bank for younger children and open a bank account for older children. Invest in their financial literacy by introducing them to online financial literacy videos for kids, buying them easy to read finance books for kids and/or enroll them in a finance class for kids to teach them about money.

Practice each of the five principles to maximize your motherhood potential. Trust your motherhood instincts, and know you are doing your best to raise honorable and successful individuals.

> Behind every young child who believes in
> himself, is a parent who believed first.
> –Matthew L. Jacobson

Motherhood Journey
Take Away Message

Think Big in setting your motherhood goals. Set aspirational goals for your children and believe in their ability to achieve these goals.

Conquer your motherhood fears by focusing on the motivations behind your goals. Focus on the progress your children are making to keep you going.

Identify and find the right knowledge to help your children achieve their goals by growing their talents and/or strengthening their weaknesses.

Find and engage mentor moms in your own mother and other moms around you who are successfully raising balanced children.

Build the whole child physically, emotionally, mentally, intellectually, socially, and spiritually.

Build confident children by complimenting your children, eliminating derogatory language, and spending quality time with them.

Build competent children by growing their individual talents and nurturing their creativity and passion.

Build resilient children by promoting physical, emotional, mental, social, spiritual, and financial self-care.

Reflections

Write down your top three motherhood
goals for the next year.

Create a plan with targeted timelines to achieve
your motherhood goals for the next year.

Write down one specific thing you gained
from this section that you can apply to
each of your motherhood goals.

Applying The Five Principles to Your Marital Journey

> Success in a marriage does not come merely through
> finding the right mate but through being the right mate.
> –Barnett R. Brickner

Lessons from my Marital Journey

Most little girls dream of getting married, so finding a life partner and getting married is a life goal for most women. Many women, including myself, find their life partner when they are young, fall in love, and have an expensive wedding yet are completely unprepared for the road ahead. As women, we are made to believe that marriage is a fairytale and the honeymoon lasts forever. Most women go into marriage not equipped to withstand marital challenges. Marriage is not taught in school—in fact, marriage is a school, and only women who are willing to be schooled are successful in their marital journey.

It is no surprise that after an average of eight years of marriage, 50 percent of all marriages in the United States end up in a divorce.[10] The topmost reason for divorce in the United States is lack of commitment. Other reasons most commonly cited for divorce are arguments, infidelity, unrealistic expectations, married too young, lack of preparation for marriage, lack of equality in the marriage, and domestic violence.[11]

Marriage is no different than any of the other life goals we have discussed so far. It starts with vision and commitment and is sustained by knowledge and action. Commitment is the willingness to do whatever it takes to make your marriage work. When you are committed to your marriage, you seek the knowledge and tools to empower your marriage. Marriage takes work, and if you are willing to put in the work, you are more likely to succeed.

Aside from being a mother, being a wife has probably been the most complex role that I have had to *grow* into. I used the word "grow" because growth is essential in a marriage. Marriage is complex because it involves two individuals from different family backgrounds coming together. In marriage, what we have in common brings us together, but we spend a lifetime navigating our individual differences to form a perfect union. To be successful in marriage, we must think of marriage as a partnership, where each member brings and leverages their own set of unique skills and personality to build a successful partnership.

---

[10] "Marriage and Divorce," American Psychological Association (American Psychological Association), accessed 2021, https://www.apa.org/topics/divorce/.

[11] "Divorce Statistics and Facts: What Affects Divorce Rates in the U.S.?," Wilkinson & Finkbeiner, LLP (Wilkinson & Finkbeiner, LLP, August 12, 2020), https://www.wf-lawyers.com/divorce-statistics-and-facts/.

My biggest mentors in marriage are my parents. I grew up in a loving nuclear family with parents who are still married after forty-five years. There was an abundance of love and happiness in my childhood. My family upbringing and the example of my parents' marriage gave me a solid foundation and affirmed my belief in the institution of marriage. Through interacting with my parents as an adult, I have learned that no one person is perfect, and marriage is about understanding, acceptance, and even forgiveness.

After graduate school, I chose a spouse with a similar family background as myself. As a young lady in my mid-twenties, I was attracted to his good looks, kind character, great ambition, and affection for me. We spent every day of our dating years together getting to know each other and having long conversations about our hopes, dreams, and future together. After two years of amazing courtship, we were married and started our life journey together. I had very high expectations for my marriage and I did not anticipate any marital challenges. After seventeen years of marriage, we have a loving home, three beautiful children, and great jobs we both enjoy but it has taken vision, commitment, and continuous action to get here.

The first ten years of our marriage was great. My husband and I loved and supported each other through everything without much struggle. About ten years into our marriage—somewhere in our mid-thirties—my husband started to experience a desire for more growth in his professional life. He wanted more in his career, and he even wanted to start his own business. After a year of planning and assessing the potential risks and benefits, my husband quit his job in the United States and moved back to Nigeria to start his own business. This business decision required him to travel internationally and be away from home three to four months at a time. Although this was a dream come true for my husband, the physical distance made it a big sacrifice for me and the children and placed a strain on our young family.

I wanted to support my husband through his new business venture, just like he supported me through my five-year doctoral program. Even though it was a joint decision for my husband to embark on this new business venture, the physical distance while raising young children made it challenging and led to many tense moments and arguments. During this period, my husband felt like I did not support his professional desires, and I felt like I did not have enough partner support at home. This challenging time led to many open conversations about my husband's professional goals and the impact of his business decision on our family life. My husband returned to the United States after three years due to unstable political and economic situations in Nigeria.

Through this challenging experience, we grew and learned that family can persevere through challenges as long as there is a shared understanding and commitment, if couples set goals and timelines together, communicate openly about their challenges, and support each other. Growth may happen at different times for each individual in a marriage, and growth sometimes requires sacrifice. A lack of flexibility and unwillingness to sacrifice have strained many marriages, and some marriages have ended in divorce.

I know that every marriage has a different challenge. Your challenge may be a lack of connection or communication with your spouse. It may be infidelity in your marriage, or financial issues due to inadequate income or loss of income. Your challenge may even be familial due to difficult relationships with yours or your spouse's extended family. Marriage is a two-way street and it takes two people to make a marriage work, so each person must own and do their part in the marriage to make it successful.

Next, I provide some practical ways to use the five principles to maximize your marital potential.

Think Big When Setting Your Marital Goals

Set high expectations for your marriage with your marital goals. Envision the type of marriage you want to have and create it. If you want a loving, committed, united, and functioning partnership, then make these your marriage goals. Identify and set your marital goals together as a couple, and identify opportunities to achieve your goals together.

Start right by choosing a spouse with the right qualities for you, and choose your spouse for the right reasons. Then believe in yourself, your partner, and your ability to create a successful marriage together.

Maintain positivity in your marriage by focusing on your individual strengths, the qualities you admire in your spouse, and the reasons you came together.

Surround yourself with successful marriages to increase your confidence in marriage. Connect emotionally with your spouse as you work through your marital goals, and check in periodically with your spouse to assess the health of your marriage.

Conquer Your Marital Fears

Admit any marital fears you have. Your fear can stem from personal experience with divorce, divorce in your parents' marriage, or in your extended family. Conquer your fears by committing to your marriage despite your fears. Commit to your marriage despite the challenges—unless you are being physically, verbally, mentally, emotionally, or financially abused. In these situations, seek help, and get out if the situation gets dangerous and threatens your survival.

Identify the motivations behind your commitment. Your motivation may be love for your spouse or wanting to be an example to your children or both. Whatever your motivations are, let them fuel your commitment to a successful marriage. Practice your commitment by prioritizing your marriage and creating time for each other regularly. Speak your commitment by speaking words of affection and affirmation to each other. Act your commitment by being affectionate toward each other.

Through any marital challenges, focus on the progress you are making as a couple and the reward of building a successful marriage together. Avoid comparing your marriage to other marriages and stay focused on your own marital goals.

Seek and Acquire Marital Knowledge

Empower yourself by seeking good quality marital knowledge. There are several great books on marriage. One that

I recommend is *The Seven Principles for Making Marriage Work* by John Gottman.

You can also attend marriage seminars, listen to podcasts on optimum marriage, and seek marital counseling if you experience marital challenges you need expert advice to resolve.

Avoid discussing your marital challenges with friends and family to prevent getting biased opinions. If you need to confide in someone, chose a close, trusted, and objective family or friend. This is because your friends and family may still view your spouse negatively long after your marital issues are resolved.

Find Marriage Mentors

Surround yourself with successful marriages for extra motivation. You may be surprised to find out that your marital challenges are not unique to you.

Learn how other couples have successfully navigated similar challenges but do not compare your marriage to other marriages. Always stay true to the uniqueness of your marriage. Adapt any lessons learned to your particular marital situation and thrive within your own marital circumstances.

Act and Follow Through with Your Marital Goal(s)

Let the change you want to see in your marriage begin with you. Sometimes you may have a list of expectations for your spouse, but you should first stop and evaluate if you are living up to the same expectations. Lead by example to create an enjoyable marital journey with your life partner

Do not leave your marriage on autopilot. Work on your marital goals just like any other life goal. Develop, document, and execute your plans for achieving your marital goals together. Execute a part of your marital plan every day to build a strong marriage. This is especially important when life gets busy with raising young children and pursuing your careers or businesses as it becomes easier to lose sight of your marital goals.

Empower your marriage by consistently practicing these essential elements of a successful marriage.

- **Love:** Love is not just the butterflies you felt in your stomach when you first met your spouse, or the smile that spreads across your face every time you see your spouse. Love is a deep feeling of emotional connection and history you share with your spouse. Show love to your spouse through your words and actions. Make your home a sanctuary of love and peace. Avoid unnecessary arguments and temptations that lead to infidelity. Loving each other regardless of life's twists and turns will keep you committed to your marriage.
- **Trust:** Trust is a necessary element for sustaining a marriage. Lack of trust can destroy any marriage. Build trust in your marriage by being transparent in all your actions and staying accountable to each other emotionally, sexually, and financially. Trusting that you and your spouse are accountable to each

other and you will not let each other down gives you the confidence to stay committed to your marriage.

- **Respect and Acceptance:** Respecting and accepting each other for who you both are is an important element of a good marriage. Many women get married to the idea of an ideal spouse. They enter their marriage with the intent of changing their spouse, then they get disappointed when, after many years of marriage, they are still complaining about the very same attributes they were hoping to change. Accepting each other's limitations and celebrating each other's gifts will keep you committed to your marriage.

- **Honest and Open Communication:** Maintain open communication in your marriage. Open communication allows each spouse to feel safe enough to express them self and know that their spouse will hear and support them. Discuss and listen to each other's needs, fears, and concerns without being judgmental. If you are unsure of anything in your marriage, ask questions rather than making assumptions. Acknowledging each other's needs and concerns shows love and will strengthen your will power to stay committed to your marriage.

- **Selflessness and Support:** Selflessness is another necessary element of a successful marriage. In a marriage, each spouse must look past their own needs at different times in the marriage to meet the needs of the family. Put each other first and support each other especially at challenging times in your marriage to increase your commitment to your marriage.

- **Patience and Perseverance:** It takes patience and perseverance to stay committed to your marriage. Develop the capability to endure difficult circumstances or accept delayed gratification without getting angry, upset, frustrated, or threatening to quit your marriage. Patience and perseverance develops over time through experiencing difficult times. If you are spiritual, trust God, and ask for patience to get through challenging times in your marriage. Patience builds endurance, and endurance will keep you committed to your marriage even during challenging times.
- **Forgiveness:** Forgiveness is a conscious decision to overcome a negative emotion from something done to you by another person and to release the feeling of resentment. Forgiveness after a negative incident like infidelity is necessary to move forward in a marriage. Seek counseling when needed to understand the root cause of the negative incident and make the necessary changes to move forward in your marriage. True forgiveness means you are starting on a new slate and you do not refer back to the negative incident when disagreements occur.
- **Gratitude:** Above all, be grateful for the gift of a life partner. Having an attitude of gratitude in your marriage allows you to focus on the positive things in your marriage. Focus on the love you have for each other. Be grateful for your partner's love, the home you built together, your children, and good health. Speak your gratitude by letting your partner know you are grateful for the partnership. Celebrate your individual strengths and work on your limita-

tions to strengthen your marriage and make your union perfect for you.

Practice all five principles to grow in your marriage. Know that you and your spouse are not the same persons you were when you got married several years back. You are growing as individuals, but you also have to grow together as a couple. Be committed to growing in your marriage and be cognizant that the timing and rate of growth may be different for each partner in the marriage.

A perfect marriage is not when the 'perfect couple' comes together.
It is when an imperfect couple learns to enjoy their differences.
–Dave Meurer

Marriage Journey Take Away Message

Set high expectations for your marriage and believe in you and your spouse's ability to create a successful marriage together.

Conquer your fears by prioritizing your marriage and committing to your marriage despite any marital fears you have.

Seek good quality marital knowledge and seek marital counseling if you experience marital challenges you need expert advice to resolve.

Find and surround yourself with successful marriages to motivate you and apply lessons learned without comparing your marriage to others.

Develop essential marital elements like love, trust, respect, acceptance, communication, support, perseverance, and gratitude necessary for a successful marriage.

Grow with your marriage and focus on your individual strengths to make your union perfect for you.

Reflections

Write down what commitment to
your marriage means to you.

Write down one marital goal you have and
document specific plans to accomplish it.

Write down the top three marital
elements you desire and will work on
developing in your marriage.

Applying The Five Principles to Your Financial Journey

> If you do not know how to care for money,
> money will stay away from you.
> –Robert Kiyosaki

Lessons from my Financial Journey

I am certainly not a financial expert, but I have taken deep interest in personal finances in recent years. I have learned a lot, and I am still learning. I realize attaining financial independence is an important part of maximizing my potential. To me, financial independence is having investments and cash flow enough to be able to retire or pursue interests that are not financially driven. I realize that to attain the level of financial independence I want for myself and my family, I have to first change both my money mindset and money habits.

Even with all my years of formal traditional education and training, I lacked the financial education to attain financial independence. Like most people, I went through a formal education, became an adult, and started making money without learning how to manage or invest money. Most people, including myself, were raised by our parents to be consumers and not investors. Due to my lack of financial knowledge, I fell into many financial pitfalls. I bought a lot of things I did not need and built up unnecessary credit card debt. Until my mid-thirties, I did not fully understand the impact of responsible financial habits on my financial credibility, like timely credit card payments and keeping a low credit card balance. It took me well into my thirties to learn that my financial habits today will impact my future financial credibility and independence.

I worked for over ten years with a decent income when it dawned on me that I could make a six-figure salary and still have no money if I did not change my money mindset and habits. It is easy to find something to buy if I do not set a spending limit, budget my spending, and pay myself first. I realize that with a six-figure salary, one can live in a nice home, drive luxury cars, and appear to live a fancy life—and still live from paycheck-to-paycheck.

One evening I was talking to my husband, and he shared with me his goal of becoming financially independent enough by fifty-five years old to pursue his passions. He asked me how I wanted to spend my time when we were no longer raising our children. I was surprised to hear he had such a plan especially because I did not have a plan beyond the typical plan to retire at sixty-two years of age with decent retirement benefits. We were making good income as a family and my husband was making sure we were putting enough money into our retirement accounts to retire successfully. Up until then, I had not even calculated how much it would take to retire with the same quality of life we have now, and I certainly had not thought about having a choice to retire earlier than sixty-two years old or envisioned what retiring earlier would look like. After a few days of mulling over our conversation, I realized my husband had tapped into a different money mindset that I was not even aware existed.

I have never learned how to invest so I had left most of our family financial decisions and planning to my husband. My husband always was more financially educated than myself, as he took a deep interest in wealth building and money management at a young age. To me, he was the *money guy* in our family as he taught me to fund and maximize my retirement investments before I ever thought about retirement and he opened college savings for our children as babies before they could even spell college. I left all our investment decisions to him and he kept me abreast of our family financial plans as needed.

Like many things in our marital life, there was a clear division of labor within our financial life. My husband did all the financial planning and I managed the day-to-day home finances. However, after that conversation with him, I knew I needed to do more to gain financial knowledge, change my money mindset, and be a full financial partner to my husband in our family journey toward financial independence.

I started to invest in my financial education by reading books and attending financial classes taught by financial experts who were teaching others how to think like and become millionaires. The most important lesson I learned is that financial independence starts in your mind and your financial thinking affects your money habits, which in turn affects your ability to build long-term wealth. Once I recognized my self-limiting financial beliefs, I was able to raise my financial consciousness, and elevate my financial thinking to envision different financial possibilities. This empowered me to start making different financial choices and decisions and create different financial habits toward our financial independence.

I started by taking stock and evaluating my income, payroll deductions, debts, and spending. Then I developed an investment plan and a spending plan. For the investment plan, I started with my retirement accounts. In one year, I consolidated my three retirement accounts into one account, maxed out my retirement contributions, and took advantage of all my agency matching. I also transferred a larger percentage of my retirement investment holdings to stocks, rather than the less aggressive mutual funds for higher yield over time. Then I opened an investment brokerage account for buying and selling individual stocks.

For my spending plan, I reviewed my spending over the previous year and categorized my spending into "need to have" and "want to have." When I first started this process, I realized there were so many things on my budget spreadsheet that I termed "miscellaneous." These were things I did not budget for, but I spent money purchasing them. These were habitual things like eating out, getting hair, nails, and eyelashes done, getting monthly facials, and vacationing multiple times a year among other things. I am certainly not against these pleasures of life, but I have learned that if you do not minimize these "want to haves" initially, you will not be able to increase your investments enough to actually afford your "want to haves" later. After cutting down my "want to haves," I had enough money left over every month to pay myself first. Paying myself first meant that I moved a specific amount of money out of every paycheck into an individual investment account before paying any of our bills. This investment account was different from our retirement accounts, emergency family fund, or our children's college savings accounts.

By taking all these steps in one single year, I doubled my retirement investments, paid down ten thousand dollars in credit card debt to zero, and started investing in individual stocks and new business ventures. Energized by my new money mindset, money habits, and how much I was able to accomplish financially in one short year, I created a freedom plan. My freedom plan includes a ten-year plan to financial independence and possible early retirement if I so choose. This journey that started with a casual evening conversation with my husband led me to envision a new financially free future. My financial education is an ongoing process and I fully expect to continue to learn, grow, and re-imagine my financial plans as I take more action to achieve financial independence.

Next, I provide some practical ways to use the five principles to set yourself on a path to financial independence and to maximize your money potential.

Think Big When Setting Your Financial Goals

Financial independence starts in your mind. Think Big in setting your financial goals. Your financial thinking affects your financial habits and your ability to build long term wealth. To achieve financial independence, you must change your money mindset first by identifying your self-limiting financial beliefs and elevating your financial consciousness by thinking like an investor.

Set aspirational financial goals and identify your one year, five-, ten-, fifteen-, and twenty-year financial goals. Start with your end goal in mind and create an investment plan to reach your desired goal. When you know your financial goals, it becomes easier to create an investment pathway to your financial goals.

Be creative in identifying different investment opportunities. Identify investment options like stocks, real-estate, and/or businesses that you understand or you are willing to learn about. Focus on potential financial rewards when choosing your investment options.

Surround yourself with people, especially women, who are financially successful for extra motivation. Tap into their financial mindset to learn how to think to become financially successful. Believe in yourself and know that if others can achieve financial independence, you can achieve it too. Later on, I summarize different investment strategies you can use to get to your financial goals.

Conquer Your Financial Fears

Acknowledge any financial fears you have. Your financial fear may stem from your childhood or young adulthood, having a negative relationship with money, or not knowing how to save or invest money.

Regardless of your level of financial knowledge, start by committing to your financial independence. Commit to learning how to grow and invest your money and getting out of the paycheck-to-paycheck cycle. Identify your motivations for financial independence and let your motivations empower you to make better financial decisions and choices.

Even for big long-term financial goals, start small by putting a specific amount of money away every month. As you watch your savings grow and you learn how best to invest your savings, you will become confident and motivated to identify different ways to make more money and better manage your money to increase your savings and investments.

Seek and Acquire Financial Knowledge

Invest in your financial education. The typical formal education does not provide the needed financial education to reach financial independence. Seek out financial knowledge from qualified financial experts. Learn proven strategies to help you make more money, better manage your money, and invest your money.

You can find in-person financial classes or online classes like wealthfit.com or chrisvirgin.teachable.com. You can also gain financial knowledge by reading and watching financial news and reading financial books. A few of my favorite financial books are *Why Didn't They Teach Me This in School? 99 Personal Money Management Principles to Live By* by Cary Siegel, *Rich Dad, Poor Dad* by Robert Kiyosaki, and *Secrets of Six Figure Women* by Barbara Stanny. You can also hire a financial planner from investment firms to guide you if you just do not know where to start.

Even with a high paying job, your income will plateau at some point, so it is important to learn how to multiple your money to generate future income and move you to financial independence. This is known as passive income and it occurs when you are not actively trading your time for money like most people do on the job, instead your money is generating income for you.

Learn to Make More Money. To become financially independent tomorrow, you have to increase your current active income. This is the money you generate every day by trading your time at work for money. If you make more money today, you are more likely to have money left over to invest tomorrow.

To increase your current income, you can ask for a raise in your current position or apply to higher paying roles within or outside of your current employment. You can diversify your income stream by taking on a part-time job or starting a side hustle using a skill you already have.

You can also pursue a higher degree to get jobs that will pay you more money either in your current field or in a different field with higher income potential. There are many online and evening degree programs that are suitable for working adults. Look for opportunities to have your classes paid for by your employer or by searching for grants and scholarships using search engines like fastweb.com and scholarship.com.

Learn to Manage your Money. You need to master your money in order to manage your money. To master your money, you need to know your numbers—gross income, deductibles, net income, expenses, debts, and savings. Your goal is to understand your deductibles (money taken out before you get your paycheck), lower your liabilities/expenses (things that take your money), and increase your income/assets/investments (things that make you money).

Avoid being a conduit for your paycheck. Start saving money today to invest in assets tomorrow. Develop a money management plan that consists of both a spending plan and an investment plan. Know that if you do not plan your spending, your spending will plan for you.

Learn to Multiply your Money. Real financial independence comes from multiplying your money and creating multiple streams of income that generate income for you tomorrow. Investment is the money you put away regularly today so it can work for you and benefit you in the future.

Many people never start investing because they think they need big money to start. Start small today and increase your investments over time. Learn to multiply your money by investing in markets you understand or you are willing to learn about.

Find Financial Mentors

Find financial mentors in your immediate environment or outside of your immediate environment online to teach, guide, and advise you financially.

Act and Follow Through with Your Financial Goal(s)

For every goal, you have to start with a plan. The same is true for your financial goal. Create a financial plan that includes spending, saving, and investing with specific timelines and execute to your financial plan.

Create a Spending Plan: Most people have a spending problem. If you are one of them, take control of your spending problem by understanding your current spending habits, reprioritizing your needs, and practicing self-control.

To understand your spending habits, go over your expenses in the previous year to understand what you are spending money on. Next, itemize your monthly expenses and divide your expenses into "need to have" and "want to have." Then, cut down the "want to have" and limit your spending to your "need to have."

Create your monthly budget to include your "need to have" and subtract your monthly spending budget from your monthly income to identify your savings opportunity.

The wins are in the margins, so decide on the amount of money you want to save every month and take this amount out of your paycheck first every month. Automate this monthly savings withdrawal by making the withdrawal transfer into a separate savings account to create consistency and separation.

Your budget is your lifestyle. Track your expenses and manage your budget closely. Monitor your checking account activities and balance regularly to stay on track. Many people create a budget but do not stick to it. If you do not stick to your budget, you will not achieve your financial goal.

Create a Savings Plan: You can split your monthly savings into multiple saving buckets such as emergency fund, short-term saving fund, and long-term saving fund.

An emergency fund is typically three to six months of your monthly expenses. These are monies that can be used to replace wages in case of a job loss or medical emergency.

Short-term savings can be used to pay off any debt you may have like credit card debt, car loans, or student loans. Making minimum credit card payments is not a good financial plan. It is a vicious cycle that only ends with you making money for the banks. Have a real plan to pay off your debt, sooner rather than later, using your short-term savings. As you pay off your debt, you will further lower your monthly expenses and increase your monthly savings. You can also use short-term savings for activities like home renovations, unforeseen medical expenses, or vacations so you do not have to put these activities on a credit card.

Long-term savings is the money you are putting away for investment purposes like stocks, real-estate, or business.

Create an Investment Plan: Every financial investment step you take today will move you one step closer to financial independence tomorrow. Diversify your investments using multiple investment vehicles. Here, I briefly describe few examples of investment vehicles.

- Mutual Funds: This is a type of stock that includes many different stocks in one fund. It is a portfolio of investments usually managed by professionals at investment firms like Fidelity and Ameritrade. Most retirement accounts and children college savings plans are typically managed in mutual funds as they are longer term investments and tend to be lower risk than individual stocks. For mutual funds, start investing early as time in the market is a key strategy for success. Set your investment goals for retirement and college and work backward to figure out your necessary monthly contributions. Many investment firms have retirement and college savings calculators on their website. Example of an online resource for college savings is savingforcol-lege.com.

- Individual Stocks: You can buy shares of specific companies by opening an online brokerage account and managing it yourself or letting someone else manage it for you for a fee. Create an investment plan that includes your investment goals, timeline to meet your goals, and the contribution amount necessary to meet your goals. Buy individual stocks while they are on sale to make more money later. Invest in companies you are familiar with and you understand their business. Track your stock gains and keep your stocks for at least a year or longer for a higher yield. Reinvest your gains to make more profit. Although individual stocks can be profitable, you can also lose money quickly, so assess your risk tolerance before investing in individual stocks.

- Real Estate: Many millionaires have made their money in real estate. If real estate is an investment vehicle you choose, enroll in real estate classes to understand common pitfalls and real estate tax laws. Decide if you want to stay local or expand beyond your immediate environment for real estate invest-ments. Find mentors in the business to guide you through the challenges and help you find investors for your real-estate business if you need it. Invest in a real estate tax preparer to help manage your taxes.

- Businesses: The best businesses solve a problem or meet the needs of customers. You can start a business using a skill you already have, as this may require less capital. You can also invest in different types of online businesses like *eBooks, courses,* and *trainings.* Alternatively, you can buy into existing businesses in the form of a franchise or you can find existing physical store fronts or online stores like *Shopify*, *Amazon*, and *Etsy* where you can sell your own physical products.

Practice all five principles in your financial journey to create a path to financial independence and build financial legacy.

Formal education will make you a living. Self-education will make you a fortune.
–Jim Rohn

Financial Journey Take Away Message

Think big and set aspirational financial goals. Change your money mindset to achieve financial independence.

Conquer your financial fears by committing to your financial independence. Let your motivation for financial independence empower you to make better financial decisions.

Invest in your financial education by learning how to make money, manage money, and multiply money.

Find financial mentors to teach, guide, and advise you financially.

Take action by creating and executing a spending plan, a savings plan, and an investment plan.

Make more money by adding a part-time job or side hustle, seeking promotions, switching jobs, or getting a higher education to get a higher paying job.

Manage your money by reducing your spending, increasing your savings, and paying yourself first.

Multiple your money by investing in markets you understand, or you are willing to learn about.

Diversify your investments in the stock market, real estate market, and business market for security and maximum gains.

Reflections

Write down your short-term, mid-term, and long-term financial goals.

Create your spending plan, savings plan, and investment plan to achieve your financial goals.

Parting Words of Wisdom

> To have more than you have, you have
> to become more than you are.
> –Saji Ijiyemi

Maximizing your life's potential is key to a happy life, but it can be a challenging and daunting experience if you do not have the right tools.

The road to maximizing your potential is not an easy or convenient road. You have to be willing to make many sacrifices along the way to reaching your goals.

Like everything in life, this is a process and it takes vision, commitment, focus, knowledge, persistence, and daily consistent action to stay on track. Sometimes you may fall off track, but make sure you always get back on track.

Throughout your success journey, practice the five principles we discussed in different areas of your life as a professional, entrepreneur, mother, and/or wife to build your confidence and competence. Over time, these principles will become your habits and empower you to maximize your potential and become an around better person.

Here is a recap of the five principles important to your success journey.

- Think big when identifying your goals. Everything starts with your mind.
- Conquer your fears by facing them and acting in spite of your fear.
- Seek and acquire the right knowledge and build the right skills to achieve your goals.
- Find mentors who have achieved the goals you are trying to achieve to guide you along the way.
- Act and follow through by documenting your goals, developing a plan, and taking daily and consistent action toward your goals.

While practicing these principles, enjoy your life, stay positive, healthy, balanced, and give back using these practical suggestions.

Enjoy Your Life

Life is a journey. As you aspire for different goals, have fun along the way. Find the little things in everyday life that make you happy. Be kind to yourself by giving yourself permission to grow. Spend each day being the best version of yourself and spend the next day being the better version of who you were the day before. Always see the best in yourself and others. Surround yourself with people who make you laugh. Laugh without hesitation and enjoy the journey to maximizing your potential.

Stay Positive

The secret to staying positive is being grateful. Focus on the blessings in your life. Be grateful for the little and big things. Foster a spirit of gratitude by maintaining a gratitude journal to regularly document your blessings. Start your day with activities that generate positive energy. Maintain positivity throughout your day by surrounding yourself with positive people and things. Expunge toxic relationships from your life. End your day with activities that relax you for a good night rest. Remember to celebrate every step on your success journey.

Stay Healthy

Commit to a healthy lifestyle by working exercise and rest into your daily routine. Eat healthy and balanced meals to keep your energy level up during the day. Get sufficient sleep to improve your concentration and productivity. Stay on top of your health by getting your yearly health check-ups and recommended vaccines.

Stay Balanced

Do not overwork yourself or become a slave to your goals. Tackle each goal in small incremental steps over time. Work smart by planning your weeks and days ahead to increase your organization and productivity. Create a daily routine and start your day early to increase predictability and reduce stress. Stay focused during your work hours and build short breaks into your day to keep you refreshed. Shut down when you have achieved your target goal for the day. Find the right balance for you and your family by scheduling social time, self-care time, and family time into your week. Schedule time off and vacation time periodically to shut-down, bond with family and friends, and rejuvenate.

Give Back

Be of service to others to find true happiness. Create change in the lives of others by giving back. Find a cause that you are passionate about and donate your time and/or money to advance the cause.

Practice all five principles and practical suggestions above to crush your goals while maintaining a healthy lifestyle. Cheers to living your best life!

> Go for it now. The future is promised to no one.
> –Wayne Dyer

Thank You for Reading My Book!

I really appreciate all of your feedback, and I love hearing from my readers to make the next version of this book even better. Please leave me an honest review letting me know what you thought of the book.

Thanks so much!
Adebola Ajao, Ph.D.

For more empowering messages, follow me on:

Instagram: https://www.instagram.
com/empowered.woman2021/

YouTube:https://www.youtube.com/channel/
UCH7B5TDKS9san0KD0bulA6w/featured

Bibliography

"Action." Action noun - Definition, pictures, pronunciation and usage notes | Oxford Advanced American Dictionary at OxfordLearnersDictionaries.com. Oxford University Press.
Accessed 2021. https://www.oxfordlearnersdictionaries.com/definition/american_english/action.

Clubbs Coldron, Alice. "How Rare (or Common) Is It to Have a PhD?" www.FindAPhD.com.
FindAUniversity Ltd., December 17, 2019.
https://www.findaphd.com/advice/blog/5403/how-rare-or-common-is-it-to-have-a-phd.

"Divorce Statistics and Facts: What Affects Divorce Rates in the U.S.?" Wilkinson & Finkbeiner, LLP. Wilkinson & Finkbeiner, LLP, August 12, 2020.
https://www.wf-lawyers.com/divorce-statistics-and-facts/.

"Fear." Merriam-Webster. Merriam-Webster. Accessed 2021.
https://www.merriam-webster.com/dictionary/fear.

Hartzell, Michael. "Howto 6 – List of Strengths & Talents You May Have." michaelhartzell.
MICHAEL HARTZELL INTERNATIONAL. Accessed 2021.
https://www.michaelhartzell.com/Blog/bid/17550/Howto-6-List-of-Strengths-Talents-You-May-Have.

"Knowledge: Definition of Knowledge by Oxford Dictionary on Lexico.com Also Meaning of Knowledge." Lexico Dictionaries | English. Lexico.com, 2020. https://www.lexico.com/definition/knowledge.

"Marriage and Divorce." American Psychological Association. American Psychological Association. Accessed 2021. https://www.apa.org/topics/divorce/.

"Mentor." Mentor noun - Definition, pictures, pronunciation and usage notes | Oxford Advanced Learner's Dictionary at OxfordLearnersDictionaries.com. Oxford University Press. Accessed 2021. https://www.oxfordlearnersdictionaries.com/us/definition/english/mentor.

"Talent." Merriam-Webster. Merriam-Webster. Accessed 2021. https://www.merriam-webster.com/dictionary/talent.

"TALENT: Definition in the Cambridge English Dictionary." TALENT | definition in the Cambridge English Dictionary. Cambridge University Press. Accessed 2021. https://dictionary.cambridge.org/us/dictionary/english/talent.

"What Percentage of Americans Have a PhD?" Reference.com. Ask Media Group, LLC, April 8, 2020. https://www.reference.com/world-view/percentage-americans-phd-2508f1120884e2a3#:~:text=According%20to%20U.S.%20Census%202013,to%20approximately%202.5%20million%20people.

Made in the USA
Middletown, DE
03 July 2023

34542119R00084